Awakening Your ORGANIZATION

Performance Acceleration in Healthcare:
Strategy – Culture – People - Process

BRAD F. POLLINS

Published in the United States of America

ISBN 978-1-961507-60-9 (SC)
ISBN 978-1-961507-58-6 (HC)
ISBN 978-1-961507-59-3 (Ebook)

Brad F. Pollins Publishing
222 West 6th Street
Suite 400, San Pedro, CA, 90731
bradleypollins@yahoo.com

Order Information and Rights Permission:

Quantity sales. Special discounts might be available on quantity purchases by corporations, associations, and others. For details, contact the publisher at the address above.

For Book Rights Adaptation and other Rights Permission. Call us at toll-free 1-888-945-8513 or send us an email at admin@stellarliterary.com.

Table of Contents

Dedication

This book is dedicated to the most important people in my life, my family. To my dads, Bernie Pollins and Bill Dye, they both instilled values, disciplines, and life practices that have continued to serve me well throughout my life.

To my brother Mark Dye, whose support, love, and his great sense of humor brighten my days.

To my children Ben, Amelia, Erika, and Curtis who taught me what unconditional love of a father truly means.

To my life partner, my soulmate, and the love of my life. Becky is a gift, an inspiration, a dedicated mother, and a loving wife. She has been accepting, encouraging and in those difficult moments in life, compassionate and supportive.

I love you all more than you will ever know.

Preface

A few years ago on Christmas Day, I received a message from my dad wishing me a Merry Christmas and telling me how much he loved me. At the time, I was living in small town in north of Atlanta, Georgia while my dad lived in Jacksonville, Florida. As it turns out, my dad was visiting a friend in Cape Canaveral, Florida for the holidays. My dad didn't realize that his voice was still recording as he was hanging up the phone on his end. What continued to be recorded was my dad saying to his friend "you can now call the ambulance".

As you might expect, I was very concerned, and I was able to discern that he was being taken to the hospital. I left immediately and drove from north Georgia to the hospital in Cape Canaveral. Upon my arrival, I quickly learned that my dad had a stroke leaving him completely paralyzed on his left side. As it turned out, cancer had metastasized to his brain.

Since I was his only family, I took a leave of absence from work so I could provide the compassionate care he deserved. Prior to this event, I had never worked in healthcare. As a result of this event, I became passionately committed to helping create and deliver performance excellence solutions to healthcare. It is my memory of his and our experiences that fuels the flame that burns within me.

Here's why. First and foremost, I loved my dad and I wanted to make a difference in honor of his memory. During the 7 weeks I cared for my dad, until his passing on February 18, I had no basis upon which to judge the quality of care he was receiving. Fair or not, my only foundation for judging was how he was being treated as a human being. Over the course of his care, I encountered hundreds of care providers – nurses, doctors, technicians, and support personnel. What stands out most was the indifference my dad and I encountered. It was as if they had been taught to keep their emotional distance from the patient and family when in actuality empathy and compassion is what we needed most. It has been said that the small things can be the biggest things. For example, I mentioned that the stroke left my dad completely paralyzed on his left side. So, guess where meals, remote controls, or call buttons were placed? That's right, on his left side.

Despite all the indifferences, there was one Neurologist in one of the hospitals who did something amazing that I will always remember – he made a personal connection with my dad. I don't know how the doctor found out about some of my father's interests. Perhaps he overheard me speaking with my dad or maybe the doctor spoke to one of my dad's friends. Nonetheless, how he got the information is unknown but what he did with the information is what made this experience so memorable. The doctor came into the room, pulled up a chair beside my dad, gently touched his hand, and began to ask my dad about World War II and engaged my dad in trivia questions about U.S. Presidents. You see, the doctor invested some time and found out that my dad was a World War II Marine Veteran and had a hobby of studying U.S. Presidents. You should have seen my dad's face – for a moment, my dad was pleasantly distracted from the disease that was ravaging his body.

From that moment, I have dedicated my professional life to making a difference in hospitals and health systems by delivering a comprehensive approach to accelerating performance. What I discovered and observed during my now 18 years of experience in healthcare is that there were and are so many organizational performance improvement practices that were, and in many cases still are, foreign to healthcare leaders. At best, and most frequently, disjointed practices, approaches, and frameworks, which were not linked in any cohesive manner, were being deployed. Many times, the hope was placed on a miracle solution or the latest fad or misplaced and antiquated approaches. Organizational impatience reigned supreme, and victory or defeat was declared way too early. The consequences were programs of the day that eroded workforce confidence, focus, energy, engagement, and discipline.

The need for a comprehensive transformation effort is paramount to achieving a strategically focused, culturally elite, highly engaged workforce and a continuous process-oriented organization resulting in next level performance. The purpose of this book is to ignite a passion for excellence in the four key elements of the Awakened Organizational Model.

Chapter 1

Introduction

"If you could hear what they hear, see what they see, and feel what they feel, would you treat them differently."

Cleveland Clinic Empathy Series

Imagine a world in healthcare where everyone is contributing their full potential self; a world where everyone is engaged and energized because they feel a special connection to the purpose of the organization; a world full of people partnering in the service of patients.

Awakening Your Organization builds on thirty years of organizational development and performance improvement experience including eighteen years working for and in over 40 healthcare organizations ranging from critical access hospitals, to large, employed physician groups, to community hospitals and health systems, to nationwide healthcare organizations.

The title of this book reflects its purpose, which is to awaken leaders to what is necessary to unlock the unlimited potential and possibilities for healthcare organizations through the synchronization of strategy, culture, people, and processes. The image on the cover of this book represents the law of roots and fruits where strength below ground determines results above ground. The roots represent the strategy, culture, people and processes in the organization and the fruits represent the outcomes the organization experiences.

Additionally, an Awakened Organization is filled with people who are optimistic, passionate, energized, results oriented, compassionate, and engaged by a powerful culture that elicits the very best in others. A positive environment suffocates toxic and divisive behaviors and an agenda for what is best for the organization and those the organization serves is followed.

Consider the multiple forces impacting your healthcare organization today – federal, state, and local policy changes; the crunch for scarce capital;

exploding technology; transparency of performance; payment for services; workforce challenges; growing consumer scrutiny; and increasing competitive forces. The scope, complexity, and pace of change today and in the foreseeable future can be overwhelming and seemingly unmanageable.

Awakening Your Organization will provide practical insights based on proven practices and approaches. The book outlines the key elements of an Awakened Organization with a particular emphasis on the vital role of organizational culture in strategy execution. The cover of this book cites the key domains that will be addressed – strategy, culture, people, and processes, which all have to be aligned and work in harmony to allow you to find and reach desired and sometimes horizons unseen. Unlike many books that are singularly focused, this outlines an approach that recognizes that there are many aspects to organizational performance excellence.

Let's begin by providing an amazing story that is a direct contrast to the experience with my father. This story demonstrates the incredible impact an awakened individual can have on a patient and family member and illustrates what every patient deserves at the bedside especially with the possibility of the darkest clinical outcome looming.

A dear friend's husband suffered an aortic dissection and found himself in the Intensive Care Unit critically ill on a ventilator for over a week. He was sedated, as he required several procedures throughout that time. His wife, who continually stayed at his bedside, observed one extraordinary nurse who provided care for him for several days in a row. Although he was consciously sedated and unable to respond, this nurse chose to talk to him throughout the day. She interacted with him as if he was awake by sharing current news events. She also consistently told him what she was doing for him, why she was doing it and provided reassuring gentle touches. She let him know how important it was for her to help keep him comfortable so he could heal. It was clear she truly cared.

This same special nurse was with him on the day he was taken off the ventilator and returned to a conscious state. After he was awake and alert, she introduced herself stating, "Hi, my name is Nicole, it is so nice to meet you". Our dear friend replied, "I have already met you. You have been taking care of me and talking to me while I have been asleep." He turned to his wife and said, "She is nice. She has been so kind to me."

The authentic connection and level of compassion demonstrated by Nicole cannot be purchased, mandated, or scripted - it only comes from the heart. What Nicole did for him was so profound he felt her connection even when he was sedated. As it turns out, compassion is not even measured on most patient satisfaction surveys. However, it is what matters most for patients and their families. Our dear friend's wife who has suffered the tragic loss of her husband after forty years of beautiful marriage will never forget this act of kindness.

Imagine that your healthcare organization is full of people who behave like Nicole – everyone would have a spirit of excellence for providing compassionate, safe, quality care, always. Several questions to consider are: 1) What enables Nicole do it while others do not? 2) What factors prevent others from behaving like Nicole? 3) Why do we tolerate anything less? 4) Did the purpose and promise of the organization reinforce the importance of the patient experience? 5) How committed was the leadership team to building an elite culture to influence the right behaviors? 6) What practices does the organization use to ensure they attract and hire elite talent? 7) Are processes that create obstacles for people identified and redesigned? The main point of this story is to illuminate that the best results are produced by the best behaviors and the best behaviors are a result of the confluence of strategy, culture, people, and processes.

To reinforce the story of Nicole, the authors of a landmark article entitled *Could Emotional Intelligence Make Patients Safer*? [1], make a compelling case that successful clinical outcomes such as safety, clinical care and the patient experience are improved when nurses process higher emotional intelligence. The article goes on to suggests that when care providers can identify emotions in self and others coupled with managing emotions during emotional situations then the care experience is improved for patients. Looking back on my experience with my dad, this is exactly what was missing from most of the staff we encountered. In fact, it was as if they were devoid of emotions, which led to the perception of a dehumanized healthcare delivery system.

Furthermore, a new scientific literature review by Dignity Health [2] shows that "delivering health care with kindness and compassion leads to faster healing, reduced pain and shorter hospital stays." These findings are also consistent with the feedback I have received from patient and family members interviewed through countless one-on-one interactions and focus groups. When asked to describe the worst and best patient experiences they had; the words used to describe the memorable positive experiences centered around empathy, kindness, and compassion whereas the worst patient experiences were bereft of such descriptions. Part of being an Awakened Organization that is patient-centric is uncovering the wants, needs and expectations of patients and family members.

This book is presented in six segments. First, a case for the complex nature of the healthcare market is made to demonstrate that there is a need for a multipronged approach to performance acceleration. In addition, a pragmatic four-domain approach is introduced. Second, an overview of the importance of setting clear direction for your organization and how to align every element of the business to that direction is provided. Third, the one thing that matters most to performance acceleration is described and techniques for strengthening this area are reviewed. Fourth, why the right people matter is explored, and the techniques and practices needed to instill high performance is explained. Fifth, the key success factors for multiplying efforts of continuous process improvement are emphasized. Finally, a summary and conclusion is offered and Call to Actions presented. These six segments are rich in detail and describe ideas, tools and activities that can be used to bring about sustainable change. Hospitals and healthcare systems will be used as the setting. The solutions are among us so as you read; think critically, reflect deeply, challenge your existing paradigms, and embrace possibilities.

I believe, as Jim Collins referenced in Good to Great [3], that "greatness is not a matter of circumstance, but rather a matter of conscious choice and discipline" and that "good is the enemy of great". I believe there are pockets of excellence in hospitals and healthcare systems across our great nation while at the same time there are enormous opportunities for the healthcare industry to become the best version of itself that can be imagined.

At the heart of an awakened healthcare organization is the patient. The patients are why healthcare organizations exists and the strategies, culture, people, and processes should be aligned to put the patient first to truly become a patient-centered organization, which includes compassionate, safe, quality care.

The ideas and observations shared in this book are not theoretical or conceptual; they are not born from academia. They are proven practices developed, adopted, honed, tweaked, and sometimes completely redesigned. The ideas are born from direct observations, interactions and from designing, developing, deploying, evaluating, and adjusting organizational development and performance improvement solutions from the front-line to the c-suite and everywhere in between.

Questions to Consider:

1. What does success look like for me after reading this book?
2. What does success look for my area of responsibility after reading this book?
3. What are the experiences you and your family would like to have in a healthcare setting, particularly when it matters most?

Chapter 2

The Case for Complexity & the High Performing Organizational Model

"Healthcare organizations are one of the most complex forms of human organizations we have ever attempted to manage."

Peter Drucker

According to PWC's Healthcast 2020 [4] "there is growing evidence that the current health systems of nations around the world will be unsustainable if unchanged over the next 15 years. Globally, healthcare is threatened by a confluence of powerful trends – increasing demand, rising costs, uneven quality, misaligned incentives. If ignored, they will overwhelm health systems, creating massive financial burdens for individual countries and devastating health problems for the individuals who live in them." This is reinforced by Nathan Kaufman, a leading healthcare futurist and strategist who states "Healthcare is fragmented, unsustainable, irrational and in perpetual disorder. The key to success is to have an organization with the competencies and agility to adapt to unpredictable industry forces."
The pace, magnitude, and complexity of change in healthcare today and in the foreseeable future is unprecedented. As an example, consider the following: patient expectations, regulations, evidence-based practices, demographics, competition, technologies, and demand for services are constantly changing.

Granted, these are generalities, so let's look at some specific statistics that reinforce the case that healthcare is arguably one of the most, if not the most, complex, and demanding industry.

1. There are 11,000 baby boomers aging into Medicare daily.
2. In 2010, the population of people 64 or older was 39.4 million; fast forward 10 years to 2020 and that number will likely rise to 53.2 million.

3. The United States currently has about 1,600 small clinics in drugstores, such as CVS and Walgreens, and that number is projected to increase to 3,000 in the next five years.
4. The cost of healthcare will jump to $4.6 trillion in 2020, up from $2.7 trillion in 2011.
5. It is estimated that 30% of healthcare spending is wasted.
6. The U.S population will grow from 310 million to 430 million by 2050.
7. By 2030, senior citizens will account for 19% of the population; today it is roughly 13%.
8. Today we have 12,600 diagnoses, 6,000 pharmaceuticals, 4,000 medical surgical procedures and the numbers are doubling every 5 to 7 years.
9. In 14 years, we will be short 125,000 primary care physicians nationwide.

Additionally, the pressures outlined in Figure 1 along with the focus on the Quadruple Aim of 1) improving the health of populations, 2) improving the experience of care, 3) reducing healthcare costs, and 4) addressing workforce burnout places additional demand on already overtaxed and overburden hospitals and healthcare systems.

Figure 1

These statistics and the Quadruple Aim focus in no way account for the enormous difficulties in healthcare and this chapter and book is not intended to do so. Rather, the purpose is to make the case that improvement efforts must be more comprehensive, coordinated, disciplined and agile to match the burdening demands of the ever-increasing complexity of the industry. There are several excellent resources, thought leaders, articles, and journals from well-respected people and institutions that can describe the comprehensive nature of the healthcare landscape. These resources outline and explain ever-changing factors such as regulation, legislation, competition, new technologies, emerging evidence-based practices, access, insurance, population health and new models of care.

With that said, the external factors, often referred to as market forces, are almost always external events that cannot be controlled. These market forces will create both opportunities and threats and how leaders anticipate, understand, and respond to the forces will place their hospitals and health systems in a competitive advantage or disadvantage.

Figure 2 illustrates how some companies' paradigm shifted other companies by being agile enough to either anticipate or take advantage of market shifts or by creating new business models and practices.

Figure 2

As an example, let's look at Blockbuster and Netflix. Who can remember the days of driving to a video and game rental store, renting a limited number of movies or games for a limited time, having to drive back to the store to return the games or videos, and if you were late, paying a late charge? In today's home movie and video game rental services on demand world, it is hard to imagine that business model working today.

That's exactly the opportunity that Netflix pursued by understanding consumer preferences and irritations. Netflix introduced an entirely new paradigm, in other words, they changed the rules of the video and game rental market. They entered the marketplace by offering to mail a video of choice directly to your home, invited you to keep it as long as you wanted, mail it back when your done and then receive your next video of choice in the mail again. And by the way, no late fees were assessed.

At its peak in 2004, Blockbuster consisted of nearly 60,000 employees and over 8,000 stores. [5] However, as a result of various factors including competition from Netflix, Redbox, and video on demand services, Blockbuster lost significant revenue in the late 2000s and early 2010s. The company filed for bankruptcy protection in 2010, [6] and, in 2011, Dish Network bought the remaining 1,700 stores. [7]

Blockbuster seemed unwilling or unable to adjust to the new business model. Perhaps they were wedded to their entrenched approach, perhaps they were unconvinced this could possibly be the future of game and video services, perhaps they were overleveraged, or perhaps they didn't have the appetite or energy to shift to the new paradigm. Whatever the reasons may be, Netflix is alive and well and Blockbuster has vanished. This is the essence of Deming's quote "change is not necessary; survival is not mandatory."

This is not just a story about Blockbuster and Netflix. It's a story about any healthcare organization any hospital or any physician practice that believes that what must have been successful in the past is what will determine success in the future. Understanding emerging trends in market forces will enable leaders to mitigate risks, pursue attractive opportunities, or create new paradigms.

Building on the Netflix and Blockbuster example, consider the emerging paradigm shifts in healthcare that must be explored. Think of it another way, what are the paradigm shifts in healthcare that have occurred in the past five years that if left unchecked would have placed hospitals and health systems at a disadvantage? This means leaders must spend time in the future and become market intimate. This reminds me of a powerful quote from Joel

Barker who stated, "the primary role of a leader is find, recognize, and secure the future." In other words, a leader needs to be able to anticipate, prepare for, take advantage of, and mitigate risks related to emerging trends; leaders must manufacture time to spend in the future. This is as true for organizations as it is for departments and service lines.

As a result of the complexity, demand, pace, and magnitude of change; it is impossible to rely on one or a handful of solutions. Many will say it's all about leadership, or it's all about culture. Some will say that structure is the most important lever while others will point to vision, goals, and strategy. Yet others will point to human capital practices or process optimization. There will be others that will point to customer intimacy practices, new revenue streams, competitor analysis, marketing, branding and sales.

The fact is that a complex organization with complicated challenges will require equally intricate and interdependent elements. The trick is to make the approach as simple, straightforward, and as repeatable as possible. This is the essence and key message of this book – *Awakening Your Organization.*

In my thirty-plus years of experience, I have been introduced to and worked with several organizational performance improvement models, many too complex and others too simplistic. I have developed, modified, and codified a model that is easy to understand and flows logically. I refer to the model depicted in Figure 3 as The Awakened Organization Model.

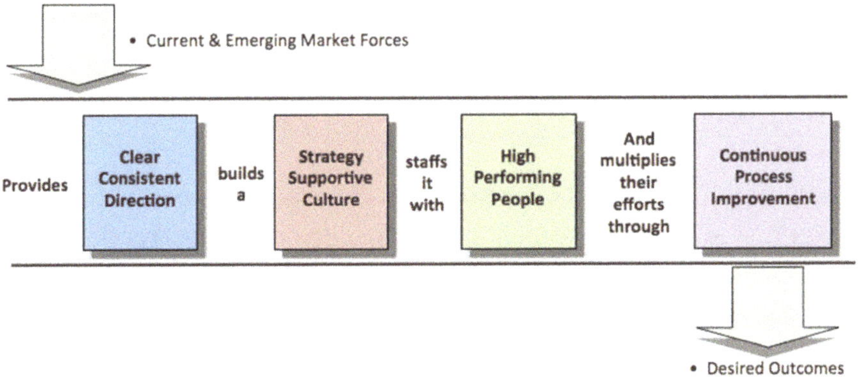

Figure 3

The model reads that an awakened healthcare organization provides clear consistent direction, builds a strategy supportive culture, staffs it with high performing people and multiplies their efforts through continuous process improvement. An organization that rigorously follows the key steps in each of these four domains will win.

Current and Emerging Market Forces is about keeping a pulse on the market environment by spending time in the future to identify, uncover and understand market dynamics. This requires a leader to spend time in the future, so the impact of emerging trends is discovered. The understanding of the market forces will allow leaders to identify potential opportunities, risks, and new paradigms.

The first domain is focused on providing clear and consistent direction. This is basically establishing a strategy that will allow a company to not only survive in the market but also win. In fact, in the simplest of terms, the primary role of strategy is to win in the marketplace. Once the strategy is developed, a continual renewal process is necessary to remain agile enough to consistently adapt to new and unanticipated changes in the business environment. In other words, the focus is to develop a market adaptive strategy. This domain also includes who needs to be involved in direction setting and who needs to understand the direction, from the Board of Directors to front-line employees and everyone in between. I have seen many strategy efforts fall short because each department, function, team, and individual did not understand their direct part to play in strategy execution. In fact, a fatal flaw I have observed in healthcare strategy is a lack of attention to alignment of all functions and individuals in their part to play, which results in silos and fragmentation leading to misfires, waste, frustration, and frankly, a lack of execution leading to desired results not being achieved.

The next domain, build a strategy supportive culture, explores the primary role of culture and the breadth and depth needed to foster that desired culture. Culture should be recognized as perhaps the most important contributor to successful strategy execution and good business performance. The behaviors, initiatives, and practices necessary for strategy execution should be promoted, practiced and reinforced because a close culture-strategy match energizes people to do their jobs in a strategy supportive manner, which promotes good strategy execution and improved business performance. Consider this, great outcomes are produced by great behavior, great behavior is driven by a great culture and great cultures are fostered by great leadership. Said another way, culture engages the behavior needed for strategy execution. With an elite culture, the old saying "culture eats strategy for lunch" can shift to *culture ensures that strategy enables performance acceleration.*

Staff it with High Performing People, the next domain, explains the role of human capital and human capital practices on organizational performance. As highlighted in *Good to Great*, the most important asset is not your people, but rather the right people. Employees need to believe in the organization's purpose, fulfill the promises, embody the values and demonstrate behaviors consistent with those values, particularly when they are on stage. People need to viscerally connect to the vision; people need to recognize their part to play and commit fully and enthusiastically to high performance standards. In return, the organization needs to embrace and implement people practices that onboard, develop, reward and recognize high performance, where performance is a function of achieving results and living the cultural standards. Consider this as a Compact between the organization and the employees.

Lastly, Multiply Their Efforts through Continuous Process Improvement acknowledges that broken or poorly designed processes are a major impediment for people to perform at their very best. These process impediments create inefficiencies, drain energy, often result in workarounds, and cause employees and customers high levels of frustration. This chapter will review the key success factors for increasing the odds of success for process improvement efforts.

Overall, performance is straightforward. Consider the performance formula (A x M x C = P), which is **A**bility times **M**otivation times **C**onstraints equals **P**erformance. This formula means that performance is a function of ability, motivation, and constraints. In other words, high performance is a result of people being extremely qualified, exceedingly energized and unencumbered by barriers.

Today, process improvement efforts come in many shapes and sizes from Lean Production, Six Sigma, PDCA, PDSA, and many others. I have observed, and do believe however, that an unnecessary level of complexity is being used in process improvement efforts in healthcare today. This complexity has in many cases caused people in the organization to resist and even reject the process improvement methods. Another mistake is not engaging people closest to the work in problem identification and solution development - after all, people do support best that which they help create.

In the following chapters, we will explore in depth each of the domains including tips, tools, activities and suggestions.

Questions to Consider:

1. What amount of time do you spend in the future?
2. Where are the sources of information I can access that provides insight into future market developments and trends?
3. How can this information be used to identify opportunities and risks?
4. What are the new paradigms emerging in my areas of responsibilities?

Chapter 3

Provide Clear Consistent Direction

"Without strategy, a leader has no thought-out course to follow, no road map to manage by, no unified action program to produce the intended results."

Arthur A. Thompson, Jr.

Providing clear consistent direction is the first step in the process. Understanding where you are, where you want to go and how to get there is the focus of this chapter. This includes crafting the direction and then engaging everyone needed to execute the strategy to reach your desired horizon.

I have had the privilege of leading, developing and facilitating nearly a hundred strategy sessions over the course of my career in healthcare. What are offered in this chapter are key findings, lessons and practices that will enable you to develop a winning strategy.

A company's strategy consists of an array of competitive moves and business approaches leaders implement to produce successful business performance. Strategy, in effect, is the playbook for strengthening the organization's market position, exceeding patient expectations and achieving performance targets.

Consider the following question - is your strategy working? Developing a winning strategy takes foresight, discipline and brutal honesty. But there are pitfalls – level of commitment, not staying the course, focusing only on lag measures, degree of misalignment, not understanding the market conditions, lack of execution accountability and distractions from the urgency of day-to-day operations.

What differentiates genuinely great strategies from adequate ones? How can healthcare executives create tangible advantages for their hospitals and health systems to be successful in an environment fraught with unprecedented change? This chapter describes a comprehensive system for strengthening your strategy development, deployment, alignment, and execution practices.

The ultimate goal of strategic planning is to recognize, find and secure the future. Sounds simple enough. But, as referenced before, the healthcare market landscape is changing so rapidly that leaders may struggle to fully understand and accurately predict the future circumstances of the market landscape.

Consider the changes in the healthcare environment during the last five years and the monumental shifts anticipated in the future. Factors, such as the Affordable Care Act, Repeal and Replace, Accountable Care Organizations, Patient-Centered Medical Homes, Critical Access Hospitals, Outpatient Services, Population Health, Telemedicine, Retail Health, Value-Based Reimbursement, MACRA, mergers, data transparency, chronic disease management, physician employment models, workforce shortages and competition continue to increase the difficulty of leading and managing the business of healthcare.

Additionally, the increasing complexity requires significantly different bandwidths in leadership talent – both strategically and operationally. There has never been a more valuable time to be able to craft and execute winning strategies. The strategies leaders decide on indicates that among all the paths and actions they could have chosen, they have decided to follow this route and rely upon these approaches.

Yet, according to Robert S. Kaplan and David R. Norton [9],

- Ninety percent of organizations fail to successfully execute their strategies.
- Eighty-six percent of executive teams spend less than one hour per month discussing strategy.
- Seventy percent of organizations do not link management incentives to strategy.
- Sixty percent of organizations do not link strategy to budgeting.
- Ninety-five percent of a typical workforce does not understand its organization's strategy.

Despite market demands for developing and executing a bonafide winning strategy, many healthcare organizational fall short. Remember, without a strategy, leaders have no thought-out course to follow, no roadmap to manage by, no unified action program to produce the intended results. I can tell you that in my experience very little time of the c-suite is dedicated to true strategic changes but rather the bulk of the time is consumed with dealing with the day-to-day operational urgent demands – particularly in large health systems where strategic decisions reside at the corporate office and not at the local level.

As mentioned earlier, nearly 90% of organizations fail to successfully execute their strategies. There are a number of hazards that lead to this including:

- The day to day requirements of managing the operations suffocates the energy, time and focus needed to execute the strategy. Many have called this phenomenon the "whirlwind" where the urgency trumps the important. The current processes are overtaxed and there is no room for anything new or different.
- When it comes to achieving the most important organizational goals, the role of the manager in the process is increasingly crucial. Yet, too often, managers are unclear about what the key goals are, how they contribute to goal achievement, and mostly, how to deal with initiative overload.
- There is a lack of direct part to play from departments and individuals understanding and knowing their specific responsibilities in strategy execution. Often times, they have not been involved in specifically identifying the behaviors and practices that must change in their area to make a meaningful contribution to strategy implementation. Not engaging employees in the process can contribute to high levels of disengagement.
- Leaders failing to build a powerful guiding coalition of change agents from key stakeholder groups who can influence needed changes to promote strategy execution.
- Some leaders/executives are unconvinced and uncommitted to the company's strategic agenda.

- Many leaders do not really understand what culture is and what is required to make it fit and healthy.
- Failing to deeply understand the market landscape including competition, patient preferences, regulatory and legislative changes, demographics, technology, and emerging practices.
- Loss of focus during implementation.
- Lack of a clearly articulated compelling purpose – why the organization exists.
- Failure to specifically describe the required behaviors for supporting strategy execution.

Let us turn our attention to a systematic approach that will help set clear and consistent direction so that your strategies attract more patients, withstand competitive pressures and strengthen its market position. Remember, the objective is to build competitive advantage by nurturing loyal patients.

Imagine that it is 1804 and you are embarking on the Lewis and Clark expedition to cross what is now the western portion of the United States. How much more successful would the expedition have been if the landscape, wildlife, temperatures, elevations, water and food sources that traversed the region were understood. Of course, these pioneers did not have access to such knowledge. After all, they were forging through uncharted territory. Now let's fast forward to today where such information does exist. If you were setting out on an expedition, wouldn't it beneficial to collect as much knowledge as possible about the conditions you and your team would encounter? How much better could you recognize, find and secure the future?

Think of it this way – different landscapes lead to different conditions, different conditions require different strategies. Once the landscape is understood, then the process of strategic planning can take place.

In healthcare today, we are seeing shifts in the market conditions that require shifts in leadership and strategy practices. Figure 4 depicts the five-phased approach to the Strategic Planning System. We will look in depth at each of the phases.

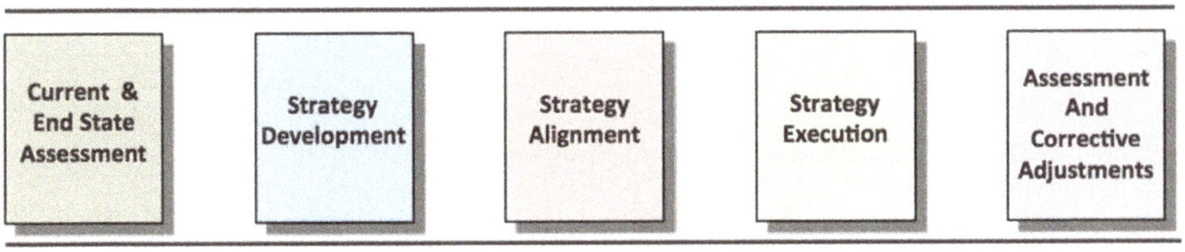

Figure 4

During the **Current and End State Assessment** phase of the system, a deep and robust understanding of the market environment is identified, both quantitatively and qualitatively. Factors such as competition, demographics, regulatory and legislative developments, emerging technologies and patient preferences are identified. The current and end state also explores compelling questions and seven areas for potential growth. The current state is further defined by completing a SWOT analysis to determine strengths, weaknesses, opportunities, and threats. The SWOT analysis provides information about 1) the effectiveness of internal processes, practices, operations and human capital, and 2) the landscape of the external environment. This phase can be likened to the diagnosis of a patient and the prescribed plan of care is only as accurate and helpful as the diagnosis. Completing the Current and End State Assessment phase will equip leaders with information on how to best navigate the landscape.

In phase two, the **Strategy Development** phase of the system, information collected during the Current and End State Assessment phase is used to craft the strategy to achieve the desired state. This includes defining the organization's fundamental purpose, promise, vision, goals and strategies. Strategic priorities are defined along with timeframes and responsibilities. To ensure momentum is created and sustained, early wins are identified. The purpose of early wins is to demonstrate to the organization's workforce that change has a high probability of success. Performance propels when everyone feels they belong to a winning team. This phase is very much like developing a treatment plan for the patient.

In the **Strategy Alignment** phase, the energy and focus is enlisting everyone in his or her part to play in strategy execution. People need to be fully energized and engaged in defining their department's contribution and their own impact on the strategic agenda. Aligning people to the strategic imperatives is accomplished by creating clear Parts to Play. Engaging people to the strategic imperatives is about involvement, being part of something special, energizing around possibilities for the company, the team and the individual. Consider this phase to be focused on fostering a strategy supportive culture. This is equivalent to fostering compliance with the treatment plan for a patient.

In the **Strategy Execution** phase, the plan is implemented. The approach that will be used to guide and keep the foot on the accelerator of execution is used to ensure a rhythm of accountability. As stated earlier, the primary purpose of strategy is recognize, find, and secure the future. Robert H. Miles of Corporate Transformation Resources, LLC [8] states "during the first full performance year under a new transformation agenda, the leader can expect to encounter no less than three predictable slumps in energy and focus, which if unanticipated and unheeded can derail the transformation effort." To minimize this reality, the Strategy System includes implementing a Strategy Oversight Team designed to ensure that focus, momentum and discipline in the execution of the strategy is hardwired into the fabric of the executives' agenda. It is critical to execute the strategy with relentless discipline while remaining flexible to adjust to changing circumstances. This phase is equivalent to the patient following their treatment plan.

Simply put, the **Assessment and Corrective Adjustments** phase tracks and reports on the progress of the strategies on the performance of the organization. Did or are the strategies achieving the intended results? The primary outcomes for this phase include: 1) success is verified and celebrated, 2) a sustainability plan is developed and implemented, and 3) an after action review is completed to compare what was supposed to happen versus what actually happened and why. With the unparalleled changes in healthcare, both in pace and scope, it is important to have a process for corrective adjustments to strategies if and when market forces demand it. This phase is comparable to adjusting the treatment plan for the patient when intended results are not being achieved.

Phase 1: Current and End State Assessment

While there are no certainties for accurately assessing current and future states, there are some techniques that will help improve the accuracy of both the current and future state assessments. First, assemble a multidisciplinary team that has the knowledge, access to information, resources, the energy and focus to provide valuable insights. Consider several multidisciplinary teams, one for each area of current state assessment. For example, current state assessment teams could be organized around the following:

1. Competition
2. Quality
3. Patient Experience
4. Growth
5. Finance
6. Community Preferences and Needs
7. Emerging Trends in Service Lines (i.e., cardiology, oncology, neurology, pediatrics, primary care, etc.).

Each team is tasked with gathering as much intelligence as possible to more accurately complete a Strengths, Weaknesses, Opportunities, and Threats (SWOT) analysis. The intelligence can be gathered from a number of thought leading sources for each area (e.g., Advisory Board, SG2, PWC, Accenture, McKinsey, Market Analysis firms, industry thought leaders, etc.).

These thought leaders might ask you to consider four important questions when analyzing current and future states. First, where do we compete (markets)? This could be geographies, product lines or services. Second, what unique value do we bring to those markets? This could be access, quality, safety, experience, medical practices, research, costs, technology, etc. Unique value is something you do in an exceptional manner that is difficult for the competition to replicate and/or barriers to entry are high for competitors. The third question is what resources and capabilities do we use to deliver the unique value? Capabilities refer to what we can do whereas resources refer to things like capital, equipment, supplies, etc. The final question is how do we sustain our ability to provide that unique value? Other potential paradigms shifting questions that could be explored in the due diligence of current and end state analysis are:

1. What anticipated market shifts will present a potentially new service line to pursue?
2. What service, done by someone else, has a market base worth pursuing that could be combined with us?
3. Who does not use our services because it is inaccessible at certain times or places?
4. What makes our services hard to access?
5. Which of my patients' annoyances should we reduce or eliminate?
6. When and why are people not using our services?
7. What benefits do my services provide that could lead to a new offering?
8. Where are we not competing where we should compete?
9. Where are we competing where we should not compete?
10. What does the Internet enable?

Additionally, the factors that will stimulate the potential for growth should be considered as illustrated in Figure 5.

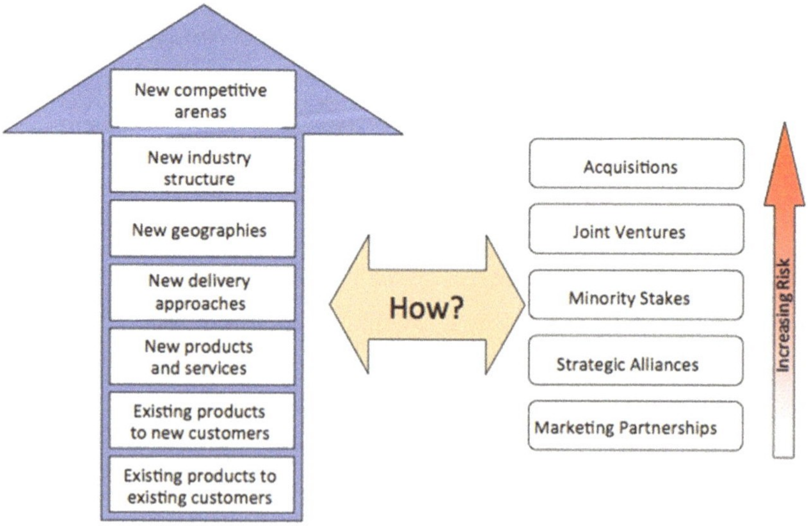

Figure 5

There are seven primary ways to growth. First, **existing services to existing patients** is the lowest-risk option; try to increase sales to the existing patient base; this is about increasing the frequency of purchase and maintaining patient loyalty. Second, **existing services to new patients** is expanding the patient base, the objective is to attract new patients to your existing offerings and then develop a long-term relationship. The third approach is offering brand new services to existing and new patients. Fourth, **new delivery approaches** focuses on the use of distribution channels as a possible source of growth. Are there ways in which existing services can be sold via new or emerging channels? Fifth **new geographies** businesses are encouraged to consider new geographic areas into which to sell their services. Geographical expansion is one of the most powerful options for growth – but also one of the most difficult. Sixth, **new industry structure** considers the possibility of acquiring troubled competitors or consolidating the industry through a general acquisition program. Finally, **new competitive arenas** require a hospital to think about opportunities to integrate vertically or consider whether the skills of the business could be used in other industries.

Now bringing our attention back to the SWOT analysis, which has two primary areas of focus. The Strengths and Weaknesses (SW) portion of the model is looking internally to the operations of the organization while the Opportunities and Threats (OT) is looking externally to the market place. Figure 6 displays the distinction between the above versus below the line focus of the SWOT analysis.

Figure 6

The distinction between operational and strategic planning is highlighted in the Table 1. The difference between strategy and operations must be clear. In fact, an idea that is rarely performed is to conduct the Opportunities/Threat (OT) portion of the SWOT first and then complete the Strengths/Weaknesses (SW) in the context of the Opportunities and Threats.

Strategic Planning	Operational Planning
• Focuses on the future – and then determines what must be done in the present to achieve the future. • Top-Down: leaders spending time in the future to identify market forces and the likely impact. • Considers changes in the market environment – social, technical, economic, political, competitive.	• Begins with the present – what we do well and not well – and focuses on how we can improve. • Bottom-Up: people closest to the work know what needs to be improved and how. • Focuses on the organizations internal structure, traditions, and practices.

Table 1

For example, after completing the OT portion of the SWOT analysis, then ask what SWs do we have that will help or hinder us in pursuing opportunities and mitigating threats? That being said, it is also important to complete the SW in isolation for the OT to ensure a deep dive is completed on what is working and not working so day-to-day operations improvement opportunities can be identified.

Figure 7 is a simple and practical tool that can be used to complete the SWOT analysis with each of the multidisciplinary teams. The teams are assembled and an experienced and skilled facilitator assists with the completion and prioritization of the items identified for each of the SWOT elements. There are a number of prioritization techniques that can be used including Paired Comparison, Grid Analysis, Urgent/Important Grid, Pareto Analysis, or Impact Analysis. Additionally, the tool allows the teams to capture the competition's strengths, weaknesses, opportunities and threats. Assessing the competition will allow you to make comparisons to your organization and the competition, which will uncover potential risks to mitigate and opportunities to exploit.

Area of Focus: Cardiology

Our Current State Assessment			
Our Strengths	Our Weaknesses	Our Opportunities	Our Threats

Primary Competition

Competition Current State Assessment			
Their Strengths	Their Weaknesses	Their Opportunities	Their Threats

Figure 7

Once the items have been prioritized, the end state, also referred to as the desired state, should be defined for each prioritized item. Next, a gap analysis should be completed to determine the reasons for the differences between the current and desired state. When completing the gap analysis, being brutally honest is imperative. The reasons (or causes) will provide insights into the problems that need to be addressed. For this to be as meaningful as possible, the end state for each prioritized item should be described in vivid descriptions so there is clarity about the destination.

The key deliverables at the conclusion of this phase include:

1. List of target areas for a SWOT analysis.
2. Multi-disciplinary teams assembled and oriented for each target area.
3. Intelligence Descriptions for each of the target areas.
4. Completed SWOT for each of the target areas.
5. Priorities for each target area.
6. An end (desired) state description for each priority.
7. A completed gap analysis for each target area.
8. Clear problem statements for each gap.
9. Root causes for each problem.

Armed with this information, the next phase, Strategy Development can begin.

Phase 2: Strategy Development

David Kryscynski explains in the video *What is Strategy* [10] that "the word strategy comes from the Greek word 'strategos', which means the art of the general. In other words, the basis of strategy comes from the art of war, and specifically the role of the general in a war. In fact, there is a famous book entitled the Art of War by Sun Tsu, a renowned Chinese general in the second century B.C. We learn from the Art of War that the fundamental purpose of strategy is to win. The role of the general, like modern day leaders, is to provide high-level orchestration and vision."

Think of businesses as modern-day war. But the casualties are more frequently lost volume, decreased revenue and damaged brands rather than human lives. The challenge of leaders today is like the ancient general. The modern-day leader needs to determine the destination of the organization, establish goals and then develop a game plan that leads to success. To establish a clear direction, the strategic plan should include the following:

1. A timeless purpose
2. A promise
3. Core values
4. A compelling vision
5. Clear goals
6. Goal owners
7. Specific strategies to achieve the goals
8. Strategy owners
9. Defined tactics to accomplish the strategies
10. A scorecard displaying the key quantifiable metrics
11. A set of shared values

Figure 8 is a visual display of the key components of the strategic plan. Let's take a look at how each element is defined.

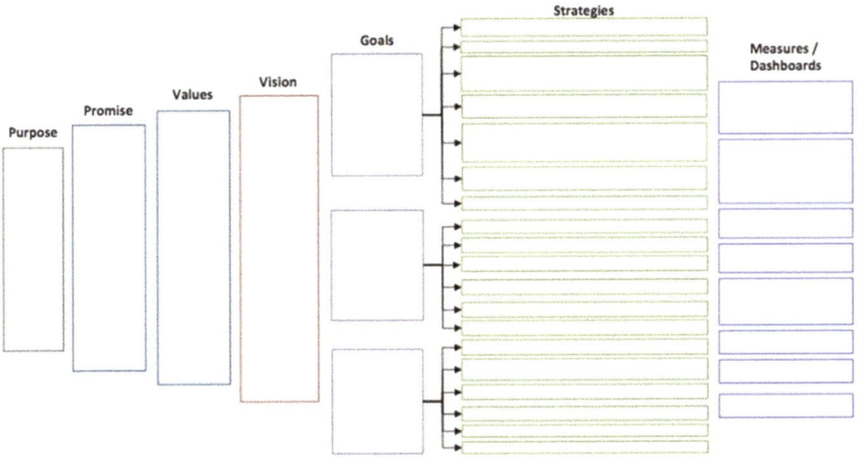

Figure 8

The purpose expresses the reason for the organization, the primary "why" the company exists. The criterion for a good purpose includes it being timeless, concise, enduring, and inspirational. As Simon Sinek points out, "people don't buy what you they buy why you do it." A great example is Disney's purpose, which is "to bring happiness to children through their imagination." This purpose applies to all business lines, departments, functions, and employees. It is expected that everyone fulfills the purpose with each guest encounter.

Imagine how your organization would perform if every one of your employees lived the purpose everyday with every patient encounter. The purpose should not, and often is, confused with vision. Remember, purpose is the why whereas vision is the overarching what. To develop a purpose statement, begin by completing this statement. The reason our organization exists is to… Consider the following examples. Our purpose is to improve the health of the citizens in our community, or our purpose is to care for you like a dear family member or our purpose is to deliver the best patient experience. A tip to consider is that the purpose is not about making money, that is an outcome, a result. The purpose should inspire minds and engage hearts like it did for Nicole in the earlier story. Let's now turn our attention to the promise.

According to *Building Patient Loyalty and Trust* in the Group Practice Journal [11] "Healthcare customers rely on personal recommendations from family and friends to judge an organization's quality of healthcare more than any other source of information." This suggests that every interaction with a patient and their family must be a memorable one. I believe it is the natural, unexpected, positive moments that generate feelings of loyalty. Often it is the compassion delivered by the caregiver to the patient that elevates respect and courtesy into something more tender and unforgettable than good routine care.

Ultimately, you want patients to be married to your brand, which turns into positive word-of-mouth advertising for your hospital, medical practice, service line or health system. But where do you begin? Begin with developing a persuasive promise to your patients. The promise is a pledge about the experience and care the patient will receive. The promise does two important things. First, it attracts new prospects and second, if the promise is accomplished, it leads to higher patient retention. The promise must be known and it must connect to 1) prospects to attract them to try your health services, 2) your existing patients to keep them coming back, and 3) your employees so they know what to deliver. Consider completing the following statement when crafting a promise statement(s), we pledge that we will... When the promise is consistently delivered, patient loyalty will be the outcome.

Core Values will be explored in more detail in Chapter 4. For now, the Core Values reflect how you need everyone to show up with each other, the patients, and the family members they are serving. The Core Values are born from the deeply held beliefs every employee should have to live the purpose and fulfill the promises.

Ask ten people to describe what a vision is and you are likely to have ten different answers. Consider your vision to be the main overarching goal for your organization, the one Big Hairy Audacious Goal (BHAG) as Jim Collins described in Build to Last. [12] A strong vision has the following qualities. A good vision sets the target, points people in the same direction, guides the use of resources, directs actions, initiatives, practices, establishes criteria for assessing progress and is time specific.

Begin by using a simple exercise. Imagine there is a feature article in the Harvard Business Review three years from now about the amazing accomplishments your health system has achieved. On the front cover of the magazine there is a headline statement introducing the article; what would you want the headline statement to read? The headline statement will provide a starting point for developing a bold vision. The vision should be expressed from an A to B by When statement. When defined this way, the vision statement will satisfy the criteria listed above.

An example of a compelling and galvanizing vision statement is from John F. Kennedy who said on September 12, 1962 "we will land a man on the moon and return him safely to the earth by the end of the decade." In this vision statement, from A equals the earth, the to B is the moon and by when is the end of the decade. A more concrete example in healthcare could be – we will move from 16% market share to 25% market share in outpatient services in the geographies we serve in five years. The advantage of this level of precision should be clear, it provides a definitive target. Expressing the vision statement from A to B by When also provides the primary measure that will be tracked and reported, namely in the example above, percentage of outpatient market share in the specific geographies served.

One of the clear mistakes that I have observed repeatedly is the tendency for people to write vision statements that are too general, vague, and qualitative thus lacking the specificity needed for people to clearly understand the target to be achieved. The same discipline in writing a vision statement applies to developing goals.

Like the vision statement, each of the goals should be written using from A to B by When structure. An example of an A to B by When goal is move from a three star rating to a four star rating in the nurse communication domain of HCAHPS in twelve months. Simply stated, the goals are the primary objectives that need to be achieved in order to attain the vision. Each goal statement should begin with an action verb. The action verb allows the intent of the goal to be clearly understood. Consider the difference between the action verbs "design" and "build". Using these two verbs to construct a crude goal, design a house versus build a house would lead to very different outcomes - a blueprint for one and an actual house for the other. The action verb leaves no mistake of interpretation behind the intent as to what is to be achieved.

Now this will come as no surprise, but one of the common observations across all the health settings I have witnessed is that hospitals and health systems are on initiative overload. Demand commonly exceeds capacity to deliver on all the "important" efforts underway. Additionally, the resources required to maintain the day to day operations – the urgent needs – are consumed leaving little time, energy and focus to work on achieving key goals, strategies and projects. In the battle between urgent and important, urgent wins the day. To combat this phenomenon, leaders must be selective and focused. In healthcare we are pursuing way too many goals at the same time. Pick the vital few goals that best support the achievement of the vision; the self-restraint to say "yes" to everything is vital. Remember it is ok to say "no" if it does not serve the vision.

Another common mistake is not aligning accountability to a goal. As the saying goes, if everyone owns it, no one owns it. Assign ownership to each goal. This is the person responsible for driving and executing the strategies and tactics needed to reach the goal.

Strategies are the specific things that need to be done in order to hit the target as outlined in the goal statement. Determining the appropriate strategies can be uncovered by looking for best practices that have worked in other settings so time, energy and resources are not wasted. It is important to understand how the A to B by When structure impacts strategies. For example, a goal to lose 20lbs in 1 month will call for a different rigor in strategies compared to the goal of losing 20lbs in 3 months.

The multidisciplinary team offers different perspectives and a richness of ideas that can be leveraged into creative strategies. Like the discipline described for goals, the key is to uncover the meaningful few strategies versus the insignificant many. The key is to avoid over burdening the organization with strategy overload. The strategies also need to begin with an action verb to clearly articulate the intention. Strategies can be converted into projects that when completed will advance efforts to achieve the target as expressed in the goal.

Figure 9 is a one-page tool that can be used to capture the key elements of the strategic plan – the purpose, promise, goals, strategies, values, and behaviors. The one-page summary can also serve as the principle communication instrument to provide clear and consistent direction to key stakeholders who will have a role in executing the needed activities to reach the goal. Just like each goal has an owner so to should each strategy, the person who is responsible for driving the strategy to completion. The core values and essential behaviors will be further articulated in Chapter 4.

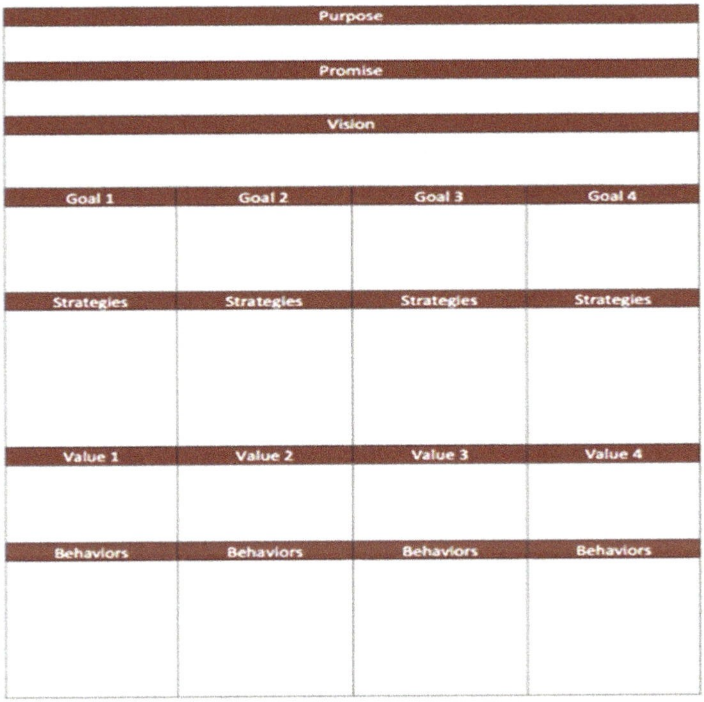

Figure 9

The next step is to develop a detailed work plan that lists the needed action steps (tactics) that will need to be completed to achieve the strategy. Figure 10 is work-planning template, which includes the list of tactics, the tactic owner, due dates, deliverables and key dependencies.

The tactics are the specific action steps that will be taken to accomplish the strategy, and yes, an action verb should be used to express each tactic. Next, the person responsible for completing the tactic is listed in the Owner column. A specific Due Date is captured for when the tactic should be completed. The Deliverable(s) are listed in the final column. The deliverables are the tangible product(s) that are produced by completing the tactic and are the evidence that the tactic has been successfully completed.

Strategy:			
Tactic	Owner	Due Date	Deliverables
Key Dependencies:			

Figure 10

The final row, Key Dependencies, reflects the resources, stakeholders and capabilities that will be needed to support the achievement of the strategy considering all of the tactics that are listed. In the absence of a specific work plan many will rely on what is reflected in Figure 11.

Figure 11

As the saying goes, if you don't measure it, you can't improve it. The role of a Scorecard is to display the progress being made on key measures. Once the vision and goal statements are expressed from A to B by When then identifying the measures is easy (i.e., volume, market share, quality, safety, revenue, expense, patient experience, brand reputation, etc.). It is a great deal more cumbersome and difficult to identify key measures when qualitative statements are used to express the vision and goals.

The scorecard should be transparent to all those involved in implementing the strategic plan and should display both "lag" and "lead" measures. The "lag" measures are almost everything that is measured and reported today (i.e., mortality, morbidity, safety, patient experience, on time first surgical case starts, volume, revenue, expense, etc.). "Lag" measures are after the fact – performance through the lens of "lag" measures is looking at what happened weeks or even months ago. On the other hand, "lead" measures are data that can be collected and displayed on a very frequent basis, daily or weekly, which are highly predictive of impacting the "lag" measure. For example, the Nurse Communication Domain is a lag measure but hourly rounding, which is highly predictive of positively impacting the Nurse Communication Domain can be measured very frequently and therefore would be a lead measure. As a reminder, the scorecard, including both lag and lead measures needs to be updated frequently and be visible to the people responsible for impacting the goals and implementing the strategies.

Before we touch on organizational values, let's take a look at the mechanism that needs to be operationalized to ensure a rhythm of accountability for implementation. At the highest level, it is recommended to create a group of senior leaders that meets monthly to review the status of the strategic plan and make any needed corrective adjustments. This team should also include the leader from each goal team. This means that there should be a goal team that meets regularly to review status, monitor progress, make adjustments, publicize and celebrate wins. Ideally, the goal teams meet prior to the senior leadership meetings so the goal leader is prepared to provide updates to the senior leader team when they meet.

I have often been asked, "What comes first, strategy or culture?" I believe that strategy comes first because it provides the clear and consistent direction of what must be done to win in the market place. The values serve to define the culture needed to support strategy execution. The role of culture then is to align, encourage and influence the decisions and actions (behaviors) required by people that contribute to the strategic intent outlined in the strategic plan. This is why values are so important. The values should express the beliefs that everyone should embody and the behaviors everyone should consistently demonstrate to live the purpose, deliver the promise and effectively carryout the strategies and tactics.

Consider this, everyone in the organization should have three responsibilities. Their first responsibility is to live the purpose. Reflect on the earlier example of Disney's purpose, every cast member should fulfill the purpose of bringing happiness to people. Similarly, everyone in your organization should behave in ways that support the purpose, always. The next responsibility is to deliver on the promise(s) with everyone the promise(s) impacts; this could be patients, family members and even each other. The final responsibility is to understand and deliver on their part to play in their job that supports goal, strategy and tactic achievement.

As an example, I remember a remarkable food service specialist who fulfilled all three responsibilities with one particular patient encounter that I witnessed while rounding. On this particular afternoon, I was visiting an orthopedic patient when the food service worker arrived. She knocked on the door, entered the room, apologized for interrupting our visit and warmly greeted the patient by name. As she entered the room I noticed she gelled in to sterilize her hands all the while maintaining her focus on the patient. With a big smile she informed the patient that his dinner was ready and asked if she could bring it to him. The patient hesitantly said yes but added that he didn't have much of an appetite because of the pain he was experiencing. Her attention immediately went to demonstrating warmth and kindness. She approached his side touched his shoulder and said, "I am so sorry you are not feeling well, I know this can be a difficult process." She went on to explain that her mother recently had knee replacement surgery and she remembered how difficult it was for her the first few hours after surgery. She then reassured him that the worst would be over soon and he would be on his way to healing. She then connected him to the importance of nourishment to his recovery. He acknowledged her and asked her to bring him the food. She brought the tray of food in, placed it in front of him, removed the lids and described what he had. She once again encouraged him to eat so he would have the energy for rehabilitation. She asked if there was anything else she could get for him, gently touched his shoulder and said I know you will feel better soon. During this encounter, I witnessed the food service specialist accomplish the three responsibilities. She lived the purpose of being safe and compassionate. She delivered on the promise of treating the patient as a dear family member and she completed her task of delivering hot food on time.

Phase 3: Strategy Alignment

As mentioned earlier, in the **Strategy Alignment** phase the energy and focus is on enlisting everyone in the organization in what his or her part to play is in strategy execution.

In providing clear and consistent direction, it is important than everyone understands his or her particular part to play, which can be accomplished by creating a Part-to-Play for each department and each individual. The Part-to-Play precisely describes the role of each department and individual, where appropriate. Figure 12 is a useful Part-to-Play tool that can align department and individual contributions.

Organizational Goal	Department Contribution	My Contribution

Figure 12

During the Strategy Alignment Phase, change management approaches are used to identify, evaluate and enlist key change agents and stakeholders in the process of strategy execution. It is also important to note that not everyone will be supportive of the change agenda as outlined in the strategic plan. Remember, new strategies are in themselves, changes that have to be made to achieve some desired result. The reactions to changes and transitions are well documented by other authors and are predictable. A number of reasons for why people resist change and therefore do not align to the strategic agenda include the following:

1. Fear of how the change will impact them or the fear they won't be able to perform
2. A commitment to doing things the "old" way
3. History of past efforts failing or not being completely successful
4. The culture is not supportive of the proposed "new" way of doing things
5. Did not understand **why** the change was being made
6. Too busy doing "the real work" – the day to day operational demand
7. Don't think that the change makes sense
8. Find it difficult to cope with either the level or pace of the change
9. Disagree with the validity of the benefits
10. Paradigms that make it difficult for people to see and understand the new rules

The fact is that during times of change peoples' attention is diverted to "me" issues such as how will I be impacted? Will I be able to perform the requirements of the new agenda? What will happen to my job? When "me" issues go up typically productivity declines. The change management efforts can help people transition to be aligned with the requirements of executing the strategy, but the most effective method is developing clear Part-to-Plays for departments and people where each strategy or action is weighted enough to guide efforts.

Phase 4: Strategy Execution

The biggest failure point of achieving the goals outlined in the strategic plan is a breakdown to execute the strategies. In other words, a loss of focus, determination, and discipline because the urgent day-to-day operational requirements suffocates the effort, time, focus and energy needed to pursue the strategies.

It is recommended that you create, operationalize, and utilize a functioning Strategy Oversight Team. The purpose of the Strategy Oversight Team is to ensure focus, momentum, and discipline in the execution of the strategy. The Strategy Oversight Team is comprised of the senior executives of the organization, and each is given responsibility for achieving a goal and implementing the strategies needed to achieve the goal. The team should meet frequently to review status, monitor performance, celebrate successes, and make corrective adjustments based on unanticipated challenges and setbacks. The Four Disciplines of Execution [13] offers wisdom and four key methods for executing during the daily operational demands. The four disciplines are:

1. Focus on the Wildly Important Goals (WIGS)
2. Focus on Lead measures versus Lag measures
3. Create a compelling and visible scorecard
4. Implement a cadence of accountability

Remember, it is critical to execute the strategy with relentless discipline while remaining flexible to adjust to changing circumstances.

Phase 5: Assessment and Corrective Adjustments

Simply put, the **Assessment and Corrective Adjustments** phase tracks and reports on the progress of the impact of the strategies on the performance of the organization. Did or are the strategies achieving the intended results? The primary outcomes for this phase include: 1) success is verified and celebrated, 2) a sustainability plan is developed and implemented, and 3) an After Action Review is completed to compare what was supposed to happen versus what actually happened and why. With the extraordinary changes in healthcare, both in pace and scope, it is important to have a process for corrective adjustments to strategies when market forces demand it.

In the Chapter 3, **Build a Strategy Supportive Culture**, we will explore the critical role of culture, why it is often said that culture eats strategy for lunch, and leading practices to foster, reinforce and hardwire key cultural practices.

A final thought on strategy, according to the American Management Association High-Performance Organization Survey [14], which "asked 1,369 respondents about an extensive series of characteristics, associated with high performance. It identified higher performers by inquiring about revenue growth, market share, profitability, and customer satisfaction. The research team correlated responses about market performance with responses relating to strategy, leadership, customer orientation and other factors, looking for the largest gaps between the highest- and lowest-performing groups.

The survey found that the single largest gap between these groups was due to whether organization-wide performance measures matched the organization's strategy. In other words, the proper alignment between performance and strategy seems to make a big difference to organizational success. The second-largest gap between higher-performing and lower-performing organizations was due to whether organizations' strategic plans were clear and well thought out. If we put these two major findings together, we see that higher-performing organizations are much more likely than their lower-performing counterparts to have clear, well-thought-out strategies that are matched up well with performance measures. This sounds a bit like Management 101, but it reveals two critical and related organizational characteristics that managers often lose sight of amid the hubbub of new business ideas: consistency and clarity."

Higher-performing organizations ensure that a strategic plan is "well thought out" because they understand that no company can perform well if poor leaders devise poorly conceived strategies. Strategic planning is a process to help with clarity and consistency so the company can win in the marketplace.

Questions to Consider:

1. Do we have a compelling organizational purpose?
2. What are our promises to our patients and to each other?
3. What is our vision and does everyone understand it?
4. Are our vision and goals expressed from A to B by when?
5. Do the goals advance us closer to achieving the vision?
6. Do we have the right strategies to accomplish the goals?
7. Do we have goal and strategy owners?
8. Have detailed work plans been developed outlining the implementation plan of the strategies?
9. How can we use Part to Play to align departments and individuals to their part to play in the strategic plan accomplishment?
10. Have we articulated values that enable strategy execution?
11. Does everyone understand they have three primary responsibilities?

Chapter 4

Build a Strategy Supportive Culture

"I came to see, in my time at IBM, that culture isn't just one aspect of the game, it is the game."

Louis Gerstner

The quote opening this chapter is particularly relevant in building a strategy supportive culture. We have all heard the cliché "culture eats strategy for lunch", and there is a reason for this, because it's true. Yet, this cliché doesn't have to be the reality, but often, when change efforts fail, it's because the existing culture stifled the actions or behaviors needed to support the strategic agenda.

However, it is referred to - culture change, culture alignment, or cultural transformation - the journey to redefine, foster and hardwire the culture needed to win is heavy lifting. The reality is that every healthcare organization has a culture - the question to ask yourself is it a culture by default or by design? A culture by default is what naturally emerges whereas a culture by design is a deliberate reconstruction of the elements that purposefully develop the desired culture needed to execute the strategy.

Culture change takes incredible discipline, focus, energy, optimism, and courage. One of the biggest mistakes I have observed are leaders declaring victory or defeat too soon. It's not surprising this takes place because of the urgent nature to win and change as quickly as possible given market demands. However, when it comes to culture change, organization impatience is the biggest enemy.

All the elements in The Awakened Organization Model are critical to success and the sub optimization of any one of them will jeopardize next level performance. Building a strategy supportive culture that encourages, engages and energizes people to perform in alignment with the purpose, promise, vision and goals is hypercritical. Culture is the great amplifier, positive or negative, of performance.

This is exactly why this book is titled *Awakening Your Organization* where the "Awakening" refers to a culture that unleashes the potential and sparks possibilities of people in the organization. More specifically, the culture refers to the values/beliefs of the people in the organization and whether these values/beliefs align with the purpose, promise, vision and goals.

Consider this, you've decided that your organization's purpose is to deliver the best patient experience and your declared promise is to treat patients like a beloved family member. For you to fulfill the purpose and deliver on the promise consistently, what do you need everyone to believe? From countless patient and family interviews and focus groups I have conducted, some core values that align directly with delivering a great patient experience would include compassion, stewardship and respect. Imagine for a moment that everyone deeply believed in these three core values and then ask if everyone deeply believed this how would others experience us?

The reason beliefs are so important is because they are the foundation to the behaviors that will be revealed and experienced by others. Beliefs influence how someone thinks, thinking generates feelings and feelings lead to an action – this action is what others observe - the behavior they experience. In other words, beliefs drive behavior and behavior is what others experience, positive or negative.

This chapter will expand on beliefs and values while also covering a number of topics needed to design, build and implement a culture including rich examples, suggestions, and activities. This chapter will address the following questions:

1. What is culture, what role do beliefs play, and what is the primary evidence of the health and fitness of your organization's culture?
2. Why is culture so important?
3. What is the process for culture transformation and the rate-limiting factors?

Before we address these questions, let us take a look at the picture in Figure 13.

Figure 13

The picture represents, unfortunately, the typical dynamics that are taking place in healthcare departments and organizations. This image has been shared many times with healthcare leaders and staff and when asked what they see going on I have been amazed at how many have said, "that's our organization". Consider the empty thought bubbles for each of the three groups represented in your organization – leaders, managers and staff. What would you say are the thoughts that reflect what is really going on in the minds of your leaders, managers and staff?

The primary question is whether or not this represents a healthy and fit culture? The obvious answer is no, which leads to the next question, what are the reasons for this level of misalignment, and in some cases, dysfunction? Consider this statement for your organization. *Culture is what people do when leaders are not present*. What are the behaviors that the people in your organization are demonstrating when their leader is not present? Are these behaviors helping or hindering the culture? How is your organization being is experienced by others when the leaders are not present?

A number of factors contribute to these undercurrents – initiative overload, miscommunication, lack of understanding the purpose, promise, and goals, mistrust, poor relationships, command and control leadership styles, conflicting signals, poorly designed processes, people being undisciplined, politics, underleveraged and overleveraged people, misaligned behaviors, etc.

When reconstructing an existing culture, the focus should be on removing what does not work, keeping that which does, and implementing new practices in the context of the strategic agenda of the organization. The best course of action is to first determine what are the core beliefs that everyone must have and embody to live the purpose, deliver on the promise, achieve the vision, and accomplish the goals. Once the beliefs are declared, the hard work to reinforce the beliefs begins.

What is culture, what role do beliefs play, and what is the primary evidence of the health and fitness of your organization's culture?

So, what exactly is organizational culture? My working definition is that organizational culture is the collective behavior of the people in the organization, shaped by beliefs, reinforced by signals, and evidenced by the experience of employees, patients, and family members. This is the baseline definition.

To define a healthy and fit culture, a few modifiers need to be added, and notice the difference. A healthy and fit culture is the collective behavior of people in the organization shaped by deeply shared beliefs aligned to the purpose, promise, vision and goals, strengthened by belief-reinforcing signals and evidenced by amazing memorable experiences of employees, patients, and family members.

By contrast, an unhealthy and unfit culture is the collective behavior of people in the organization shaped by various beliefs misaligned to organizational priorities, reinforced by conflicting signals and evidenced by a variety of experiences for employees, patients and family members ranging from positively memorable to positively awful. So, if you want to know how healthy and fit your culture is, look to the experience others have with your organization. Table 2 provides additional evidence of a healthy and fit culture compared to an unhealthy and unfit culture.

Healthy and Fit Culture	Unhealthy and Unfit Culture
• Low turnover from high performers • Higher percentage of engaged versus disengaged employees • Signals aligned to the declared values • No boundaries • Minimal politics • People focus on what matters most to the organization • High energy and contagious enthusiasm • Flow of innovation and ideas • High productivity • People are optimistic and open hearted • Solution orientation mindset • Spend time on what is working • Recognize what others do well	• High turnover from high performers • Higher percentage of disengaged versus engaged employees • Signals misaligned to the declared values • Several silos • High degree of politics • People focus on what matters most to them • Low energy and contagious negativity • Innovation and ideas stifled • Low productivity • Lower mood states • Problem oriented • Spend time on what is not working • Find fault in others

Table 2

At the core of culture, behavior is driven by beliefs. Beliefs influence how we think about a situation, how we think about the situation produces a feeling and the feeling leads to an action (behavior). Your organizational values express what you need people to believe that support your purpose, promise, vision and goals. The people who share your beliefs will act in ways that advance your organization to the desired level of performance. There are four key elements that shape culture – beliefs, shared values, behavior and signals. Using the previous example of purpose to deliver the best patient experience, these four elements could be expressed as follows:

1. **Belief:** Patients should be treated with empathy and compassion
2. **Shared Value**: Compassion
3. **Behaviors:** Everyone makes a personal connection with warmth and kindness to patients and family members.
4. **Signal:** Leaders care deeply for and show a personal interest in their employees.

The challenge is that too many times the linkage between values and strategy execution is missed. Furthermore, there are likely, and quite unintentionally, conflicting signals that can erode or contradict the culture that has been declared as necessary to win. Signals can take many forms and usually show up in the following areas:

- **Leadership Behavior**: The leaders behavior, including the decisions made, need to be aligned to the values stated otherwise employees will receive contradictory signals. When stated values and leadership behaviors differ, the behavior of leaders will be the primary influence on others. Also, what leaders tolerate has an enormous influence on the culture. Remember, what is permitted persists. When behaviors are tolerated that are inconsistent with the stated values then the culture is compromised. Great leaders zero in on culture because they understand that the way people behave determines the performance of the business. Therefore, great leaders create a culture that energizes behavior that produces the desired results.

- **Policies/Rules**: The policies, particularly Human Resource policies, send signals that may be incongruous to the stated values. A critical review of all policies should be conducted and revised to ensure the policies align and reinforce the organizational values.

- **Structure**: The way in which an organization is structured influences how silos emerge, which can lead to detrimental boundaries. How functions are organized within the hierarchy of the organization sends signals to employees as to what matters most – be sure that what matter most is reflected in the structure of the organization.

- **Accountability Standards**: The accountability standards, what people are held responsible for accomplishing and how much the standard is weighted, guides where employees spend their time.

- **Processes**: Poorly designed processes and the unwillingness to find better ways to organize the work creates barriers to high performance. Chapter 5, Multiply Efforts through Continuous Process Improvement will expand on the role and importance of efficient and effective processes.

- **Attitude:** A healthy and fit culture in many ways is all about attitude. William James, over a century ago, said, "The greatest discovery of this generation is that a human being can alter their life by altering their attitude." I believe this to be true for reaching a healthy and fit culture as well. We can alter the culture and therefore the experience employees, patients and family members have by making a personal choice of how we show up.

Listed below are a few attitude-gauging questions to consider because the answer to these questions impacts the quality of the work environment and how well positioned you are to deliver a strategy supportive culture. Now, I must warn you, some of the questions may make you a bit uncomfortable but your honest answer to each question will provide valuable insight into how you are influencing the culture or your work area and the organization. Ask yourself…

1. How did you choose to show up today?
2. How have you contributed to the culture today?
3. What behaviors did you role modeled today? Positive or negative ones?
4. How would you describe your attitude today? Is your attitude worth catching?
5. Has your behavior improved the work setting or has your behavior contributed negatively to the work environment?
6. Have you lifted the moods of others?

These are important questions because the answers provide insight and self-awareness about how people are contributing to the culture. Every one of us owns how we show up - it is quite simply a choice. So, let's begin with where you should begin – with the focus on contributing to a healthy and fit culture. Day in and day out, what sort of example do you set? Are you personally a role model for the purpose and promise? Does your behavior influence others positively… or do you somehow influence them negatively? Consider how many people take their cue from you and ask yourself what kind of influence you carry?

So we face an important choice every moment of every day: What attitude will I choose today? Will it be one that contributes to a healthy and fit culture? It's an important choice – one that profoundly influences the culture of a department and organization. Remember, each person influences the culture by his or her attitude and actions. This is an important point because organizational transformation cannot occur without personal transformation.

The key question about signals is, does leadership, policies, structure, accountability standards and attitude trigger the best in others? For a patient first orientation, every touch-point matters from when the patient arrives to after the patient leaves and everything in between as depicted in Figure 14. As an example, the signals should be evaluated and adjusted at each touch-point to ensure consistency in the experience. When a patient and family member experience a signal that is counter to the stated values then living the purpose of delivering the best patient experience is unachievable.

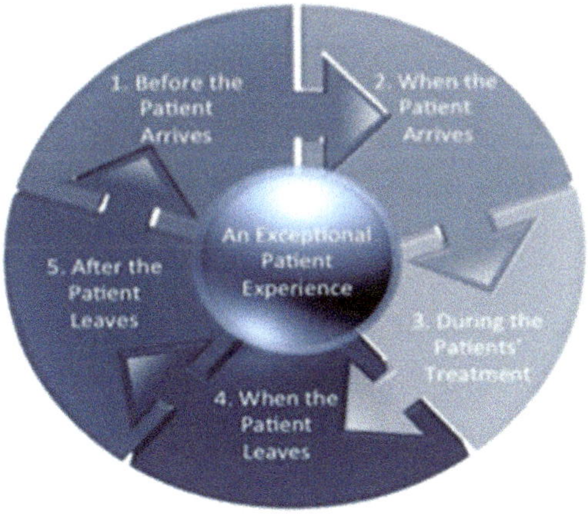

Figure 14

Why Is Culture So Important?

Culture is an important contributor to successful strategy execution and good business performance because the actions, initiatives and practices called for in a strategy may or may not be compatible with the organization's culture. This is often overlooked but the reality is that a close culture-strategy match energizes people to do their jobs in a strategy supportive manner, which promotes good strategy execution and improved business performance. When a well thought out winning strategy is combined with a healthy and fit culture then the organization awakens to incredible possibilities.

A healthy and fit culture engages and energizes the people to behave in strategy supportive ways. The connection between strategy and culture becomes clearer in this context – for successful strategy execution people must behave in a strategy supportive manner.

Another reason culture is so important in healthcare is because culture drives the behavior that patients and family members experience. Scott Louis Diering, M.D. [15] stated "our patients will know what's in our heart from the expression that's on our face...by sharing their face, we will share their heart."

I am reminded that in our world of healthcare, patients and family members are struggling with fear, pain, loss, and sadness. It is at these defining moments that caregivers provide expert medical care. It is also critical to have a culture of empathy and compassion during the patient's battle. Empathy allows people to connect with patients and their family members by feeling what they are experiencing. Compassion is love in action. It is the choice to make a difference by sacrificing personal comfort and convenience to help relieve the suffering of another. The following story illustrates this point.

A seasoned nurse who works in the Emergency Department at a large facility shared this story with me. She expressed how upset she was about an experience one of her patients had that was unnecessary and could have been avoided. The care team involved in this situation was the Emergency Department physician, the admitting Hospitalist, another seasoned nurse, and herself. They were standing outside the patient's room discussing the best possible course of treatment for a very ill patient. Unfortunately, the conversation became somewhat heated, could easily be perceived as argumentative and had a tone that the patient was an inconvenience for the care team.

While the conversation was taking place, the nurse happened to look at the patient lying on the stretcher and noticed a tear rolling down his cheek. It became apparent to her that the patient had been intently listening to the team's conversation. She decided the best course of action was to break away from the team and make her way into the room to comfort the patient. She shared with her patient that she would be his eyes and ears and ensure the team would take great care of him. Later, she shared this experience at an emergency department committee meeting. When she shared what the patient experienced, silence took over the room. A few moments later, another nurse who had recently traveled out of town on vacation stated, "On vacation, I was treated so nicely, and it was as if everyone wanted me to be there. She then asked, why is it so difficult for us in healthcare to do this with people that are sick?"

This was a pivotal moment for this team, and they decided to develop a team compact, as it had to start with them first. Their commitment was to be polite and professional with each other to have positive interactions with those they serve. They decided that they would do this by consistently acknowledging each other every day and say hello with a warm smile. The committee then shared the compact with the rest of the team, and as you can imagine, it was met with some cynicism. The team did as they were told and said hello to each other, but it became clear that it was not coming from a place of sincerity. The committee had lengthy ongoing conversation about their team culture and decided they would stay the course and be the change they wanted to see in others. After several months they began to observe a shift in the mood of the team. The number of positive team interactions was increasing, and the once fake smiles were now coming from their hearts.

The team has recognized that leadership could have told them to be nice and not have negative conversations in front of patients but that would not have necessarily caused them to change their behavior. They realized that they had to discover on their own and decide to own it themselves. This story reinforced how something so simple as a warm smile and sincere hello with each other not only can have a dramatic change on the health of a team's culture but also can translate into significant patient experience improvements. This team has experienced a significant improvement in their patient satisfaction scores.

In countless patient and family interviews and focus groups, the differentiator in creating an exceptional patient experience is overwhelmingly empathy and compassion. So, in healthcare, one of the primary reasons culture is so important is to ensure patients and family members experience empathy and compassion.

What is the process for culture transformation and the rate-limiting factors?

The approach to culture transformation is the step-by-step process of reconstructing an existing culture by removing what does not work, keeping that which does and implementing new practices in the context of the strategic agenda of the organization. New practices refer to human resource customs, signals, processes, structure, leadership, and accountability standards, which has been briefly addressed.

Additionally, Figure 15 illuminates the new mindset, a new way of thinking that contributes to building a healthy and fit culture. The shift from the old thinking to the new thinking creates a new paradigm for culture transformation, which may be counterintuitive to past models, methods and approaches to culture change.

Old Paradigm	New Paradigm
• Leadership style direct command/control	• Leadership style of stewardship & inclusion
• Behavior will change with a tell approach	• Behavior will change when those closest to the work are part of the solution
• Initiative overload	• A model of focus and discipline
• Leadership model non inclusive of physicians	• Dyad leadership model
• The importance of IQ	• Importance of EQ
• Care team centric	• Patient centric
• Focus on volume	• Focus on value
• Focus is on fixing the patient experience	• Focus is on fixing the culture by connecting the hearts, minds and souls of care team and patient experience naturally happens
• We can rehabilitate everyone	• Not everyone is coachable

Figure 15

The transformation approach that will be described on the following pages requires courage and resolve because the existing culture will push back hard on the new practices and signals that need to be reconstructed to become healthy and fit.

The shift required in thinking, behaviors, practices, and signals is demonstrated in Figure 16. As the culture transformation moves from where it is today to where it needs to be tomorrow, new thinking and behaving must be defined and changed for both leaders and staff. Moreover, current thinking and behavior that does not serve the purpose, promise, vision and goals must be abandoned – in other words, discard what no longer works. At the same time, current thoughts and actions that do serve the strategic agenda need to be retained and reinforced – keep what is currently working.

Figure 16

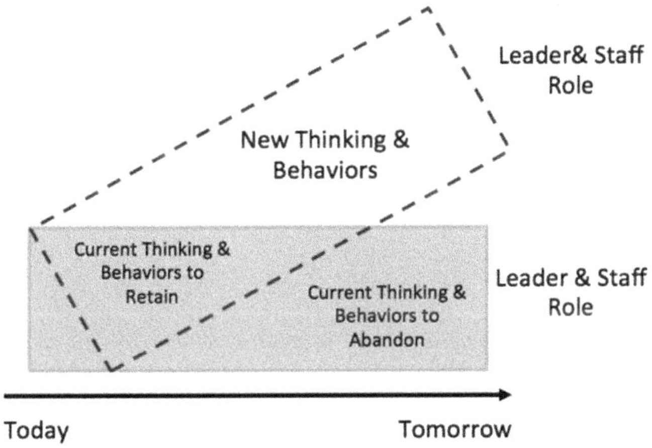

In a groundbreaking January 2010 Harvard Business Review article, *Accelerating Corporate Transformation (Don't Lose Your Nerve!)* [16] Robert H. Miles identifies *a* number of thought-provoking findings that directly apply to an effective and sustainable culture transformation process. The rate limiting factors as cited in the article include:

Cautious Management

When the transformation effort begins, people are usually absorbed in activities that reinforce the existing culture. Miles points out that people are busy in a "deep routine of doing their own thing, supporting their own slice of the organization, and getting rewarded for it. There initially is no incentive to speak out with big bold ideas to support the new transformation challenge. Contributing to this initial pattern of avoidance is fear about the unknown, the unproven and the incomplete. Managers and employees have arrived at the moment of transformation challenge by successfully mastering the competencies required by the business model being replaced. Finally, most have seen managerial initiatives and mandates come and go; so there will tend to be now of transformation launch a vein of uncertainty that runs throughout the organization about the leader's commitment to stay the course."

Business-as-Usual Management Process

The "Whirlwind", the daily operational demands, suffocates any new transformation efforts because the energy, focus, and time are overburdened leaving little room for anything new.

Initiative Gridlock

Today's healthcare organizations are experiencing initiative overload, and as a result, demand exceeds capacity on a regular basis. One can easily observe and hear about the accumulation of layer upon layer of initiatives. Miles states, "Sometimes this happens because of the proliferation of uncoordinated functional initiatives, in which each department attempts to drive improvements from its perspective throughout the enterprise. In other instances, initiative gridlock emerges because the leader of the enterprise lacks the courage to focus his or her organization on a few important initiatives."

Recalcitrant Executives

Many senior leaders remain committed to and convinced that longstanding leadership and management practices, which proved successful in a different time, will continue to be successful in the future. Many of these executives are unwilling or unable to see the new culture paradigm. In the article Miles points out that "Protracted tolerance of nonaligned, uncommitted, or incapable leaders can most certainly derail any transformation attempt. This is particularly the case of very senior executives who hold sway over large parts of the enterprise and whose skills at their advanced career stage may sometimes be out of sync with those required by the transformation agenda. Many of these key executives will loathe altering the regimes they are already pursuing in the part of the organization for which they are responsible."

Disengaged Employees

Several studies, particularly by the Gallup Organization, have demonstrated the impact and cost of disengaged and actively disengaged employees. This employee disengagement is at the heart of the saying "culture eats strategy for lunch" because disengaged behaviors defeat culture transformation efforts. Miles reinforces this by stating, "Managers and employees do not understand the need for transformation. They do not grasp the new strategy and transformation agenda. They may work hard, but do not know where to best focus their efforts. They often don't feel safe in sharing new ideas. They don't believe they will be rewarded for their mastery of new skills required by the transformation."

Loss of Focus During Execution

According to Miles, "By the time the transformation process shifts into execution, some executive leaders may have become lulled into a state of exhaustion. They may wish to think that all that positive energy and intense focus achieved during the planning and launch phase will automatically be transferred and retained during the execution phase. Falsely reassured by this assumption, such leaders all too quickly delegate the transformation oversight and follow through to others before moving on to more immediate or novel challenges."

Miles goes on to say that "during the first full performance year under a new transformation agenda, the leader can expect to encounter no less than three predictable 'slumps' in energy and focus, which if unanticipated and unheeded can derail the transformation effort just as surely as any of the five inhibitors encountered during the planning and launch phase.

The first predictable slump is the '*Post-launch Blues,*' which involves a desire on the part of leaders to relax immediately following a bold launch. After several months of distraction from their involvement in transformation planning, some executives reach their limit in being able to juggle their responsibilities for planning and launching the transformation while running their part of the day-to-day business. So, you are likely to hear something soon after launch like, 'Hey, we're over the hump!' For many this will signal their return to business as usual, which everyone in their part of the organization will surely notice and imitate.

The second predictable slump, *'Mid-course Overconfidence,'* will predictably emerge about halfway or two-thirds of the way through the first performance year. By that time, the transformation vessel will have cleared the harbor, many important things will appear to be on course, and the tendency will be to set the sails, lash down the tiller and sit back to enjoy the smooth sailing. This kind of early complacency can sap important energy and focus so critical to keeping the transformation momentum on pace and on course.

The final predicable slump comes at the end of the first performance year. Called the '*Presumption of Perpetual Motion,*' you know when you are approaching this slump when you hear something like, 'We don't have to go through all that again, do we?' This slump is based on the belief that by year-end things are progressing so well that there is no need to re-examine, re-plan and re-launch the effort at the beginning of the next performance year."

Any one of these rate-limiting factors can hinder and even defeat culture transformation efforts. A comprehensive and deliberate approach is required coupled with leadership clarity, courage and determination. Figure 17 outlines the four-phased approach to define and transform the culture at every level of the organization.

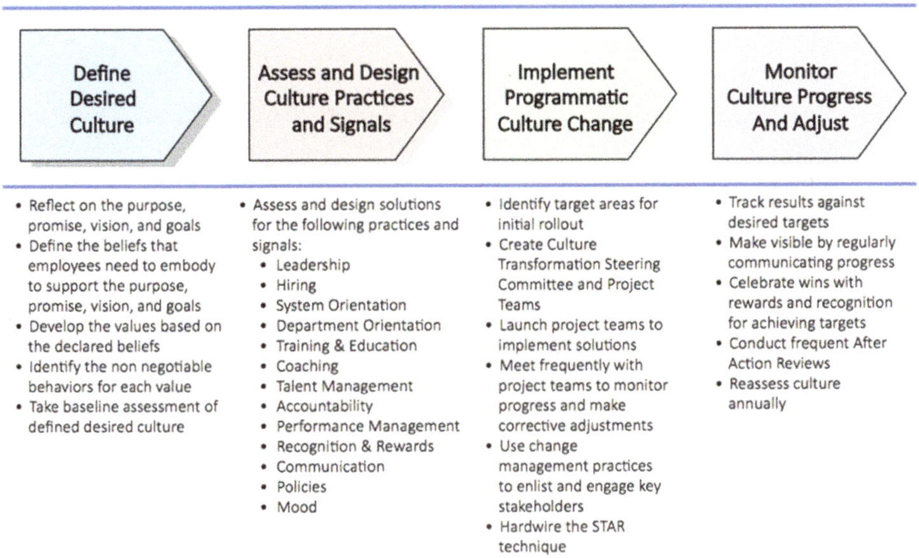

Figure 17

As mentioned earlier, the culture transformation process is the step-by-step method of reconstructing an existing culture by removing what does not work, keeping that which does, and implementing new practices in the context of the strategic agenda of the organization. Let's now look at each of the four-phases of the culture transformation process.

Define Desired Culture

In phase one, Define Desired Culture, a focused effort to think about and identify what it would look, hear, and feel like, in vivid terms, when everyone is living the purpose, fulfilling the promises, achieving the vision, and accomplishing the goals is pursued. The next step is to describe what everyone must believe at their core to live up to the vivid descriptions. The core beliefs are then converted to the uncompromising core values that the organization holds most dear. Next, and this is the most tricky and difficult step, identify the essential behaviors, the non-negotiables that everyone must demonstrate. Defining behaviors is tricky because all too often the things described as behaviors are not actually behaviors. Behaviors must be specific and observable; what you can see someone do and hear someone say. It is recommended that no more than three essential behaviors be described for each organizational value. An example of an unsuitable and suitable behavior description is listed below.

- Unsuitable Behavior Description: Treats the patient with courtesy and respect.
- Suitable Behavior Description: Make eye contact, smile, introduce yourself by name and position, and ask how may I help you?

The reason that the first example is unsuitable is because there is room for misinterpretation. What exactly does courtesy and respect look like? What some believe is respectful may not be what the patient or family members believes is respectful. Plus, courtesy and respect have different meanings. The suitable example leaves no room of interpretation, it's clear, specific, and observable.

The next piece is to assess the current state of the culture by using the Culture Quotient (CQ) assessment tool shown in Figure 18. The output of this assessment will provide insight into the overall health and fitness of the existing culture. The statements used in the assessment should be developed from the essential behaviors identified for each core value.

Additionally, employee engagement surveys should be used to assess the level and percentage of engaged, disengaged, and actively disengaged employees. Most importantly, the employee engagement survey should include a section on the experience the organization is delivering to the employees.

Culture Quotient

	Rating Scale									
	Never	Rarely		Sometimes				Freqently		Always
Behavior Statements	1	2	3	4	5	6	7	8	9	10

Figure 18

Likewise, patient experience data should be collected and analyzed to determine the patients' perception of their experience with the organization and the degree of loyalty the patient has to the organization. Notice that I didn't say to measure and collect data on patient satisfaction, and this is quite intentional. That is because merely satisfied patients will defect to the competition more easily whereas loyal patients not only keep coming back but also generate growth through positive word of mouth advertising. Loyal patients are disciples for the care and experience provided.

Assess and Design Culture Practices and Signals

In this phase, key practices and signals are assessed and redesigned to align to the declared culture as expressed in the core values and essential behaviors. Remember, the best behaviors produce the best results because how people behave creates the experience for employees, patients, and family members.

The practices and signals will empower, invigorate, and link people to what is important to achieve the desired results, or the practices and signals will disempower, disengage or disconnect people. The practices and signals take many forms, some obvious and others much less discernible. The primary practices and signals that need to be assessed and redesigned are leadership, hiring, orientation, training and education, coaching, talent management, accountabilities, performance management, rewards and recognition, communication, policies, and mood. These practices and signals will be addressed in more detail in Chapter 5, Staff it with High Performing People so for now a short description of each will be provided.

Leadership

How leaders lead, the style that they use, the importance they place on core values and essential behaviors, the way they provide feedback, what they tolerate and the experience they create for their employees is perhaps the most important practice and signal of all.

Hiring

We should never compromise on making the best hiring decision possible. As the metaphor goes, if you need eagles, hire eagles, don't hire turkeys and expect them to soar like eagles. There is not enough training, motivation or coaching that will ever enable turkeys to soar like eagles.

Orientation

The messages in system and department orientation should absolutely be consistent and aligned to how things are done in the organization. How often have we heard about an employee going through the hiring and onboarding process to be massively disappointed when he or she arrives at their department only to find something very different from what was described upon hire? This disconnect sends a clear signal to the employee about how things are really done here.

Training and Education

Technical and cultural competency development matters because it enhances the skills, capacity, knowledge, and bandwidth of people. These developmental events also need to reinforce and promote the desired culture. How many training or educational events have employees completed that immersed people in the core values and essential behaviors in your organization?

Talent Management

For the purposes of this book, Talent Management refers to the right people in the right roles at the right time. How many times have you experienced someone being over or under leveraged? Talent Management is about matching the energy and mental capacity of the individual to the complexity of the role or situation.

Accountabilities

The accountabilities, performance standards or performance goals should be focused on three primary responsibilities – living the purpose, delivering the promises, and fulfilling the job requirements. Additionally, the performance goals should align with what the organization is setting out to accomplish. In other words, the individual goals should support the department objectives, which in turn should assist with the organizational targets and strategies so there is a direct Part-to-Play as mentioned earlier.

Performance Management

The primary role of performance management is to ensure that people deliver on their three primary responsibilities. This includes providing support, resources, capabilities and eliminating constraints to performance. Most performance management approaches tend to be punitive in nature, which does not draw out the very best from people. Feedback on performance should be frequent, targeted, and specific by highlighting strengths, overcoming barriers, and coaching for improvement. A monthly one-on-one session with staff guided by a purposeful agenda is a great method for keeping the pulse of performance in departments. Also reconsider reframing this from performance management to performance stewardship.

Rewards and Recognition

Compensation, rewards and recognition models should be designed to be commensurate with performance and value delivered along with exemplifying the culture of the organization. The number one reason why people leave an organization is feeling unappreciated. As the old saying goes, "what gets rewarded gets done."

Communication

During times of change and transformation, the most effective communication is face-to-face and two-way. In today's world of electronic devises and platforms, dialog is becoming a lost art when it is needed most. One of the biggest reasons why people resist change is because they didn't understand the reason, or the why, for the change. Many communication channels must be used, and important messages repeated.

Policies

The rules that people must follow are outlined in organizational policies and governed by human resources and corporate compliance. In my experience, many policies, which leads to high levels of bureaucracy, are systematic of an undisciplined leadership team. Many policies in healthcare are required to meet the substantial regulatory requirements; after all, healthcare is the second most highly regulated industry next to nuclear power. However, too many policies exist to govern behavior, which in most cases is born from a few people making mistakes resulting in everyone being punished. The policies, as they are written, may be in direct contradiction to the culture being created.

Mood

Mood is probably the least understood and yet most impactful to the tone and style of the organization's culture. Mood refers to the emotional state, in other words the feelings, of employees throughout the organization. Consider the following two questions. Do your employees go home feeling better about their workday more often than feeling bad? Or do your employees go home feeling bad about their workday more than feeling good? The signals employees receive have a direct impact on their mood. The signals should energize, engage, and connect employees to what matters most.

The power of mood is demonstrated in the following story that was shared with me from one of the kindest physicians and who is well known in the community for her impeccable reputation. Before she shared her experience with me about one of her patients, she prefaced the conversation with "this is not one of our proudest moments". Apparently one of her patients called the office complaining of foot pain and was scheduled for an appointment with the office nurse practitioner. When the patient arrived for the appointment, for unknown reasons, the front office staff labeled the patient as a possible drug seeker. The staff passed their assumption onto the medical assistant that would be rooming the patient for the nurse practitioner. Unfortunately, the medical assistant shared this same assumption with the nurse practitioner. The nurse practitioner examined the patient and stated she did not see anything wrong with him and therefore chose not to treat.

A few hours later the patient called back to the practice complaining that he could not stand the pain that he was experiencing. The staff now admits this reinforced their original belief. This time the patient was scheduled for a follow up appointment with the physician. The same rendition of sharing the possibility of the patient being a drug seeker was repeated with the physician's medical assistant and the physician herself. The physician stated, " I saw the patient and didn't see anything wrong so I also chose not to treat. I did, however, order some blood work. Later that night when I received and reviewed his blood work, his uric acid was at a very high level. The patient had a severe case of gout and we did not treat his pain".

I share this story because it is our thoughts and beliefs that drive how we feel about situations and it is our feelings that drive our actions. Our mood plays a critical role in not only shaping how we show up relative to creating an exceptional patient experience but has a direct impact on patient safety and quality outcomes. The care team, based on their assumptions, limited their ability to seek to understand and obtain all of the information necessary to accurately assess and diagnose the patient.

Implement Programmatic Culture Change

Implementing programmatic culture changes is where the heavy lifting begins and endures. This is not a few months exercise and not a sprint but rather a marathon filled with head winds and tail winds, ups and downs, celebrations and setbacks. This is where committing to the destination, making adjustments, publishing short term wins and acting with courage, clarity and conviction is required. There will be temptations to question the effort, compromise on standards and abandon the journey. But you must remain steadfast and unwavering because the reward of a strategy supportive culture is the key to sustainable high-level performance.

It is ill advised to attempt a "big bang" rollout approach for several reasons. Start small and in the areas that are most important to the culture shifts. Focus first on the areas that have the biggest contribution to the outcomes you are seeking. For example, if the patient experience is important, and by patient experience I mean safety, quality and the patients' perception of how they were treated as a person; then pick the areas that contribute to these most.

Another reason to start small is to build positive momentum for the culture change. All too often people are beleaguered because of initiative overload and past failed change efforts, which erodes confidence in new change attempts. Positive momentum serves another purpose as well, it is the foundation for creating critical mass and serving as a "Pull" versus "Push" effect. Basically, a "Pull" effect is when people are drawn to be part of the movement, they become committed to being part of something special whereas a "Push" affect is when people are forced to be part of the change and the best to expect is compliance to the new agenda. Ask yourself this; do you want people acting out of commitment of compliance? The difference is significant; it's like the difference between an owner, a renter or a squatter.

The final reason to start small is reality of scarce resources – time, energy, money, focus and capacity. Over time, with positive momentum and the "Pull" effect, more people will enlist as change agents and cultural champions, which will help manufacture additional resources for the cause.

A Culture Transformation Steering Committee and project teams will need to be formed to develop and implement the solutions needed to address new practices and signals designed in phase 2. The Culture Transformation Steering Committee should comprise of 8 to 12 key leaders, both formal and informal, who have credibility, energy, discipline, courage and who believe in the culture transformation program.

The Culture Transformation Steering Committee should develop the overall program plan, provide resources and air cover and remove obstacles for the project teams. The Steering Committee should meet monthly to review the status of initiatives, provide direction, make key decisions, challenge existing paradigms and make corrective adjustments along the way. Also, each Culture Transformation Steering Committee member should play the role of an initiatives champion.

A project team for each of the key practices and signals should be developed with clear roles and responsibilities. The key roles should include a champion (Steering Committee member) a leader, a planner and a scribe.

Once the project teams are formed and roles determined, the team should develop a rollout approach for their solution(s). This should include a detailed workplan listing key activities, deliverables, due dates and an owner for each action step. The owner is the person responsible for implementing the action step. The project team should also have regular meetings to assess progress and drive execution of the plan. After the planning is complete, the project team implements the necessary steps for completing the new practices and signals.

Additionally, the Culture Transformation Steering Committee and the project teams need to develop a change management approach to enlist and engage key stakeholders in the process. This includes a robust and comprehensive communication strategy that includes identifying the key audiences, the messages that each audience needs to receive, the timing of the messaging and the best mechanisms to deliver the messages.
The process just outline probably sounds familiar because it is essentially the approach described for developing a strategy to achieve a particular goal. In fact, one of the key goals of the organization should be related to elevating the Culture Quotient of the organization.

Finally, hardwiring a simple yet profound technique will enable people to respond effectively to situations, both small and large. The technique is named STAR and the formula is S x T x A = R, which stands for **S**ituation times **T**hinking times **A**ction equals **R**esults. Here is how it works; a situation happens, a thought about the situation arises, the thought provokes a feeling, which leads to an action, and the action produces a result. As stated earlier, the best results are produced by the best action or behavior. Unfortunately, when a situation occurs people don't typically stop and think - given that situation what result do I want? What typically happens is there is a circumstance, we make a quick choice and there is a consequence – either positive or negative. Using the STAR technique to become a STAR performer will be expanded upon in Chapter 5.

Monitor Culture Progress and Adjust

This phase of the culture transformation process is likened to an annual physical examination with your primary care provider. The annual exam tests key markers from laboratory results to determine your overall health and fitness. From the lab outcomes, the physician suggests adjustments that should be made in health habits to improve and sustain health. The same rigor needs to be applied to culture transformation except the assessment and corrective adjustments need to be more frequent than an annual physical.

The culture performance results that are being tracked should be reported and made visible through regular communication techniques. Early wins and successes are acknowledged, celebrated and rewarded. After Action Reviews are used to determine 1) what was intended to happen, 2) what actually happened, 3) what was the difference between what was supposed to happen versus what actually happened, and 4) what changes need to be made to continue to move forward in a positive direction.

Culture is the quintessential element that drives engagement, energy, focus and commitment to the strategic itinerary. It is the DNA of the organization and everything, positive or negative, flows from it. A healthy and fit culture encourages peoples' behavior, which produce results. An unhealthy and unfit culture leads to underperformance and experiences that do not generate loyalty from employees, patients or family members. Of all of the elements in The Awakened Organizational Model, culture is the one that will determine how well a strategy is operationalized and executed.

Throughout the journey of successfully implementing the strategy, there will be defining moments for decisions and actions. The core values should be used as a moral compass to make the right decisions and take the most effective actions. When the values are compromised so is effective strategic performance.

In closing the culture chapter, I am reminded of a beautiful story entitled "*The Cab Ride*" [17], which makes me wonder what can possibly be learned from a cab ride that applies in healthcare?

"*I arrived at the address and honked the horn. After waiting a few minutes I walked to the door and knocked... 'Just a minute, answered a frail, elderly voice. I could hear something being dragged across the floor. After a long pause, the door opened. A small woman in her 90's stood before me. She was wearing a print dress and a pillbox hat with a veil pinned on it, like somebody out of a 1940's movie. By her side was a small nylon suitcase. The apartment looked as if no one had lived in it for years. There were no clocks on the walls, any knickknacks, or utensils on the counters. In the corner was a cardboard box filled with photos and glassware.*

'Would you carry my bag out to the car?' she said. I took the suitcase to the cab, and then returned to assist the woman. She took my arm and we walked slowly toward the curb. She kept thanking me for my kindness. 'It's nothing', I told her... 'I just try to treat my passengers the way I would want my mother to be treated.' 'Oh, you are such a good boy, she said. When we got in the cab, she gave me an address and then asked, 'Could you drive through downtown?'

'It's not the shortest way,' I answered quickly... 'Oh, I don't mind,' she said. 'I am in no hurry. I am on my way to hospice. I looked in the rear-view mirror. Her eyes were glistening. 'I don't have any family left,' she continued in a soft voice... 'The doctor says I don't have very long.' I quietly reached over and shut off the meter. 'What route would you like me to take?' I asked.

For the next two hours, we drove through the city. She showed me the building where she had once worked as an elevator operator. We drove through the neighborhood where she and her husband had lived when they were newlyweds. She had me pull up in front of a furniture warehouse that had once been a ballroom where she had gone dancing as a girl. Sometimes she'd ask me to slow in front of a particular building or corner and would sit staring into the darkness, saying nothing.

As the first hint of sun was creasing the horizon, she suddenly said, 'I'm tired. Let us go now'. We drove in silence to the address she had given me. It was a low building, like a small convalescent home, with a driveway that passed under a portico. Two orderlies came out to the cab as soon as we pulled up. They were solicitous and intent, watching her every move. They must have been expecting her. I opened the trunk and took the small suitcase to the door. The woman was already seated in a wheelchair. 'How much do I owe you?' She asked, reaching into her purse. 'Nothing,' I said. 'You have to make a living,' she answered. 'There are other passengers,' I responded. Almost without thinking, I bent and gave her a hug. She held onto me tightly.

'You gave an old woman a little moment of joy,' she said. 'Thank you.' I squeezed her hand, and then walked into the dim morning light... Behind me, a door shut. It was the sound of the closing of a life. I didn't pick up any more passengers that shift. I drove aimlessly lost in thought. For the rest of that day, I could hardly talk. What if that woman had gotten an angry driver, or one who was impatient to end his shift? What if I had refused to take the run, or had honked once, then driven away? On a quick review, I don't think that I have done anything more important in my life. We're conditioned to think that our lives revolve around great moments. But great moments often catch us unaware - beautifully wrapped in what others may consider a small one."

The Cab Ride connects us to a profound feeling of empathy and a desire to act compassionately. The point of the story is that patients may not remember exactly what you did, or what you said, but they will always remember how you made them feel.

A healthy and fit culture is the great accelerator to performance, particularly when, as Simon Sinek reminds us, the organization is filled with people who believe in the cause of the organization.

Questions to Consider:

1. Is your culture aligned or misaligned to supporting the strategic agenda of the organization?
2. Are the core values of the organization born from the beliefs that everyone must embody to live the purpose, deliver on the promises, and achieve the goals?
3. Have essential behaviors for each core value defined?
4. What is your Culture Quotient?
5. What current signals help and hinder progress?
6. What role does mood play in the style of the organization's culture?
7. How does the transformation rate limiting factors appear in the organization and how will the rate limiting factors be addressed?
8. Is a rigorous and disciplined approach being used to navigate the culture transformation process?

Chapter 5

Staff it with High Performing People

"Those who build great companies understand that the ultimate throttle on growth for any great company is not markets, or technology, or competition, or products. It is one thing above all others: the ability to get and keep enough of the right people."

Jim Collins

The third element of The Awakened Organizational Model is to staff the company with high performing people where high performance is a function of two critical components – producing results and living the culture.

To produce results and live the culture, a high performing individual lives the purpose, delivers on the promises, embodies the values and fulfills their job duties, which means people have to be both technically and culturally elite. An individual who is technically elite performs their job duties at an exceptionally high level. They have the knowledge, skills and abilities that are required of their particular job. To be culturally elite, people exemplify the behaviors reflected in the core values and they make others around them better by the way the show up through their attitude and actions, which requires a high level of Emotional Intelligence (EQ).

The stark reality is that people performance drives organizational performance. This is the reality for all organizations, particularly in health care where services are provided 24 hours a day 7 days a week for 365 days a year. Performance at medical facilities begins and ends with people – physicians, nurses, associates, volunteers and partners. Consider this, day in and day out it is people who take care of patients, administer medications, perform life enhancing and saving procedures, complete examinations and tests, respond to codes and deliver compassionate care to patients and their families.

To deliver the absolute best care and experience to the patient, talented people who are highly engaged in their work are needed.

Employee engagement is vitally important to the organization because there is a direct relationship between how engaged an employees is to the performance they deliver. More specifically, highly engaged employees are committed, both emotionally and intellectually, to the purpose, promise, vision, values and goals of the company.

Engagement can be seen as a heightened level of ownership where each employee wants to do whatever they can for the benefit of the patients and for the success of the organization as a whole. The Gallup organization has identified three categories of engagement:

- **Engaged** employees work with passion and feel a profound connection to their company. They drive innovation and move the organization forward.
- **Not-Engaged** employees are essentially "checked out." They are sleepwalking through their workday. They are putting in time, but not enough energy or passion into their work.
- **Actively Disengaged** employees are not just unhappy at work; they are busy acting out their unhappiness. Every day, these workers undermine what their engaged co-workers accomplish.

All too often, many of human resource practices undermine engagement because they focus primarily on the technical aspect of performance and pay little attention to the cultural qualifications. This is evident in sourcing, hiring, appointment, development, compensation, recognition, leadership and accountability practices where technical requirements are primarily stressed.

In this chapter, we will spend the bulk of the time emphasizing the need for high levels of cultural competence and the practices needed to ensure people are aligned to what matters most. Consider the following:

1. Why is the need for the right people so important?
2. What is the connection between culture and people?

3. What does being a STAR performer mean and what are the eight great characteristics of a STAR performer?
4. What are woodpeckers and how do you detect them?
5. What are the people practices that influence employee performance and how to transform them to achieve cultural excellence?

Why is the need for the right people so important?

One of the most important findings in Good to Great by Jim Collins [18] is that "people are not your most important asset, the right people are." The case for why the right people and people practices matter is illustrated in Figure 19.

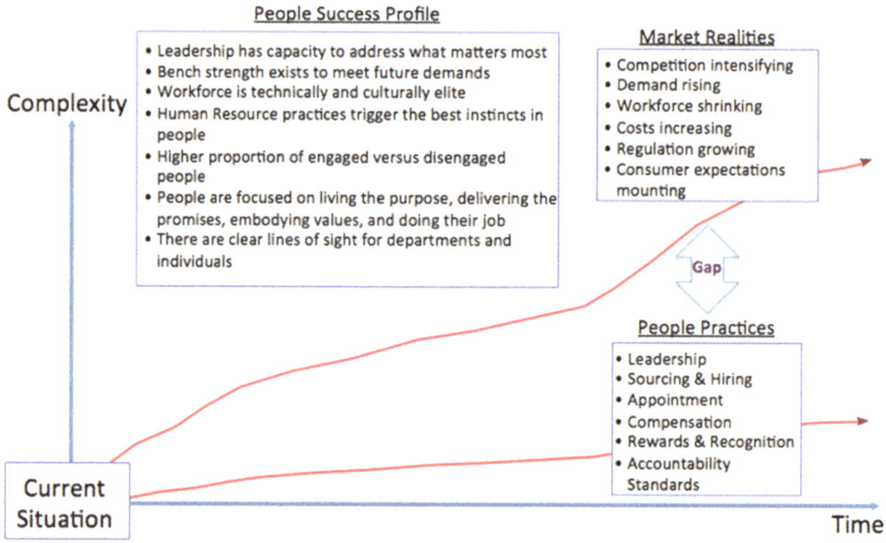

Figure 19

Overtime, the complexity of the healthcare industry is increasing due to a number of market realities including intensifying competition, rising demand, increasing costs, mounting patient expectations, shrinking workforce and growing regulation. As the complexity has and will continue to increase over time, a growing gap has emerged between the people practices that worked in the past versus the practices that will be needed to ensure success as describe by the features of a People Success Profile, which includes:

- Leadership has capacity to address what matters most.
- Bench strength exists to meet future demands.
- Workforce is technically and culturally elite.
- Human Resource practices trigger the best instincts in people.
- Higher proportion of engaged versus disengaged people.
- People are focused on living the purpose, delivering the promises, embodying values, and doing their job.
- There are clear Part to Play for departments and individuals.

Consider that the organizations' performance is the direct result of employees' performance – it is people who make decisions, take actions and behave in ways that produce outcomes. The result of these decisions, actions and behaviors will determine the results the company will experience. A senior executive once asked, "When will we see results improve?" I replied, "When people change their behavior."

Employee engagement continues to be a struggle for most organizations. There are a number of studies that still show that the percentage of disengaged employees outnumbers engaged employees resulting in lost productivity estimated to be in the billions of dollars. The implication of course is that attaining organizational goals is at risk when employees are not psychologically invested in the organization or motivated to contribute to its success.
Mike Packnett, CEO of Parkview Health stated, "Without employee engagement, you're never going to get the kind of ultimate patient experience you're hoping for." In the article, *The ROI of Employee Engagement in Hospitals* [19], Kevin Kruse, the author, points out that "Many people make the mistake of confusing employee engagement with trying to make workers satisfied, or even happy." The article makes the distinction between a satisfied nurse and an engaged nurse where a satisfied nurse shows up on time without complaint and does the minimum required and yet they may very well be happy at work. Conversely, a nurse who is engaged commits fully to the job; gives their discretionary effort and acts in ways that serve the purpose, promise, goals and core values of the organization. The article cites the following examples of signs of discretionary effort:

- The engaged hospital worker makes eye contact with all visitors and escorts lost family members to their destination
- The engaged caregivers never forgets to wash their hands or check IV lines
- The engaged worker notices the yellow 'fall risk' bracelet on a patient in the lobby and helps her back to her room
- The engaged care giver listens, unrushed, as patients ask about their medications and discharge orders
- The engaged night-shift workers are mindful of being quiet
- The engaged food service worker ensures all meals are accurate to dietary restrictions and delivered while still hot
- The engaged nurse always rounds on the hour
- Engaged workers takes care in checking and double-checking medication order before administering
- The engaged healthcare worker provides comfort and kindness to a patient that is emotionally anxious

In addition to engagement, elite talent is critical to a company's competitive advantage particularly in highly complex departments. It should be noted that departments are not created equally in there complexity to manage and lead. For example in healthcare, a function's difficulty is influenced by volume, regulation, medical complexity, patient acuity and ratio of leaders to employees just to name a few. Appointing people with the right talent and engagement level is crucial to strategy execution and culture transformation. High performing people are very talented, highly engaged and deliver results while exemplifying the culture. Appointment strategies, that is matching the talent level to the complexity of the job, is a strategically important workforce management imperative.

So, the business case for having the right people, behaving in the right ways, making the right decisions and taking the right action becomes clear in the context of performing at a level that leads to winning in the market place. People, above all other factors, impact the success of the business enterprise.

What is the connection between culture and people?

The connection between culture and people is straightforward. The culture of the organization is what others (patients and employees) experience from interacting with people in the company. As mentioned in Chapter 4, a healthy and fit culture is the collective behavior of people in the organization shaped by deeply shared beliefs aligned to the purpose, promise, vision, and goals, strengthened by belief-reinforcing signals and evidenced by incredible memorable experiences of employees, patients and family members.

The connection between people and culture should be clear – people, through their decision, actions and behaviors produce the culture. In other words, every person in the organization contributes to the culture, positively or negatively, based on how they show up. People who live the core values elevate the culture and therefore the experience that others have with the organization.

To illustrate how employees impact culture and the patient experience consider the following story that a family member who works for a large health system shared with me. My family member was scheduled for a quick appointment at his primary care physician's office for an immunization. When he arrived for his 11:00 a.m. appointment, the employee at the front desk greeted him. The employee asked for his name and upon looking at the office schedule quickly stated, "Your appointment is not at 11:00 a.m. it is scheduled for 4:00 p.m.". My family member stated "No, I had it on my calendar for 11:00 a.m.". The exchange of who was correct went back and forth until my family member said they would just come back. Although he agreed to come back he couldn't help but think in the time it took to debate the appointment time he could have received the immunization. As he approached the elevators he encountered two other patients having a conversation.

The one patient said that she had an appointment, which turned out to be at the same practice, and when she arrived they informed her that the appointment was not schedule for today, it was scheduled for next Friday. The other lady standing beside her stated "Oh that has happened to me too". My family member, as a devoted employee of the health system, introduced himself and asked how he could help. With one simple question and about a two minute conversation with the patient at the elevator here is what he learned. The patient had a neighbor drive them about 45 minutes to their appointment. She stated she was in so much pain she did not know how she was going to be able to wait another week to be treated. She also shared that when she call earlier in the week to schedule the appointment the scheduler asked, "How does Friday sound?" Unfortunately, the date of the appointment was never exchanged. My family member escorted the patient into the clinic and was able to help the staff understand the situation and of course when they did, they quickly chose to do the right thing and work the patient in for an appointment.

I know if the employee focused on truly seeing the patient as opposed to their task at hand they would have done the right thing the first time. It only took one look to see this little old lady who not only stood hunched over her walker but also had an expression of utter disappointment. High performing people, particularly in healthcare must improve their emotional intelligence so they can be more aware of and respond to the emotions in others. All too often, I have observed healthcare employees being so focused on completing tasks that they forget the primary reason they are there – to focus on both the medical and emotional needs of the patient.

A healthy and fit culture, encourages, enables, engages and energizes people to perform in a strategy supportive manner. Therefore, leaders set the direction to win in the market place, foster a culture that enables strategy supportive behaviors, ensures people are selected, developed, encouraged and rewarded for being both technically and culturally elite.

As referenced in the Figure 18 from the previous chapter, the overall health and fitness of the existing culture is reflected in a customized Culture Quotient (CQ) for your organization. A list, roughly three, of essential behaviors should be identified for each core value. These vital behaviors become the basis for the personalized Culture Quotient Survey. The output of the survey will determine the health and fitness of the culture.

That being said, it should be noted that when people are rushing, frustrated, fatigued, or complacent culture weakens, performance suffers and the opportunity for mistakes increases. As an example, I want you to imagine for a moment that you are patient in an inpatient room on a medical/surgical unit.

When the caregiver enters the room, they are either rushing, frustrated, fatigued or complacent. Could you tell? What behaviors would you observe? How would it make you feel? What do you think your experience would be? Would you feel that safety and quality care were at risk?

In healthcare, the certainty is that people are often rushing, frustrated, fatigued or complacent due to a number of factors. This erodes the culture that you are trying to create thereby impacting the perception of the patients' experience. The reasons for why people are in these emotional states need to be uncovered and addressed to become culturally elite.

Table 3 is a useful tool for uncovering the impact of the four critical emotional states that erodes the culture and therefore the patients' experience. For each of the emotional states identify the behaviors that are observable when someone is rushing, frustrated, fatigued and complacent. Next, pinpoint the likely impact the behavior is having on the culture and the patients' perception of their experience plus the likely mistakes that could occur. Then, isolate the root causes for each emotional state, and finally, determine the remedy, the solutions, for addressing the causes to reduce people feeling rushed, frustrated, fatigued, and complacent.

Factor	Rushing	Frustrated	Fatigued	Complacent
Behaviors				
Impact				
Causes				
Remedy				

Table 3

What is a STAR performer and what are the eight great characteristics of a STAR performer?

Being a STAR performer means being able to effectively respond to situations that produce the best results. As a reminder, the STAR formula is S x T x A = R, which stands for **S**ituation times **T**hinking times **A**ction equals **R**esults. Remember when a situation happens, a thought about the situation arises, the thought leads to a feeling, the feeling produces an action and the action produces a result. Everyone in the organization needs to be familiar with and master the use of the STAR technique to equip him or her to better manage the situations they encounter at work. The good news is that the behaviors identified for the CQ will provide insight into how someone should respond to situations.

For example, let's imagine that a nurse encounters an angry patient because of an excessive wait time to see the physician. The angry patient is the situation. Once the situation occurs, the nurse begins having thoughts about the angry patient. The thoughts will be influenced by a number of things including past experiences, frustrations, workload, fatigue and prejudgments, which determines the Focus Frame of the nurse. The Focus Frame is the self-talk or story the nurse tells himself about the situation based on past history. The story the nurse tells himself produces a feeling and the feeling leads to an action/behavior. The formula is lightning fast – the situation occurs, a thought is formed, a feeling emerges, an action occurs and a result is produced.

Often, people act very quickly to a situation giving little thought to the result they want. If the nurse does not use the formula like a STAR performer, the likely outcome will not be in alignment to living the purpose or delivering the promises. STAR performers use the formula this way. When a situation happens, the STAR performer asks what results do I want given this situation? Once they are clear on the result they want they then select the best action/behavior needed to produce the desired result. In this example, let's assume that compassion is a core value and a list of critical behaviors has been identified to demonstrate compassion. If the STAR performer's intended result is for the patient to feel heard, valued and cared about, what behavior can the nurse demonstrate to achieve this desired outcome?

Non-STAR performers are typically on autopilot and do not readily think about the outcome they want given a particular situation – they just respond, which can lead to unintended negative results. At the extreme end is how a victim thinks about the STAR formula. Victims usually blame the result on the situation and take no ownership on how they think and act in the situation.

The STAR formula is a valuable technique for achieving improved results given all situations that are faced. However, not all situations are created equal in terms of their importance. When the stakes are high, using STAR technique effectively is even more essential.

STAR performers also share the following Eight Great Characteristics. STAR performers:

1. Care deeply
2. Make a genuine connection
3. Spark the best and lifts the moods in others
4. Demonstrate enthusiasm, optimism and seek possibilities
5. Stay focused on making the important things matter most
6. Build trust and social capital through high quality relationships
7. Provide solutions
8. Respond to adversity with resilience

Care Deeply

STAR Performers care deeply about living the purpose, delivering the promise achieving the vision and accomplishing the goals. They also care deeply about results, serving others, supporting their colleagues and attending to their own well-being. In healthcare, STAR Performers care deeply about the care and experience of their patients by imaging the patients they are serving as a dear friend or family member. In this way, empathy and compassion naturally flows from this visualization. They understand that caring is the ultimate connector because it creates an emotional association with people. They find out what is important to the other person and they make it important to themself as well. Caring deeply is important because it promotes making a genuine connection.

Make a Genuine Connection

When STAR Performers care deeply, they make a genuine personal connection with others. Caring guides the way STAR performers listen. In the absence of caring, people don't listen for all the facts and feelings; they listen with an eye towards formulating their own response. STAR Performers understand that communication is essential to high performance because they know that communication connects them to co-workers, patients, friends and family members. When they listen more carefully, they are able to identify small nuances – tone and body language that impacts their perception of the message being received. Additionally, one who cares deeply delivers their message more thoughtfully.

A simple yet powerful tool to use to make a personal connection with a patient is reflected in the All About Me section of the Whiteboard displayed in Figure 20.

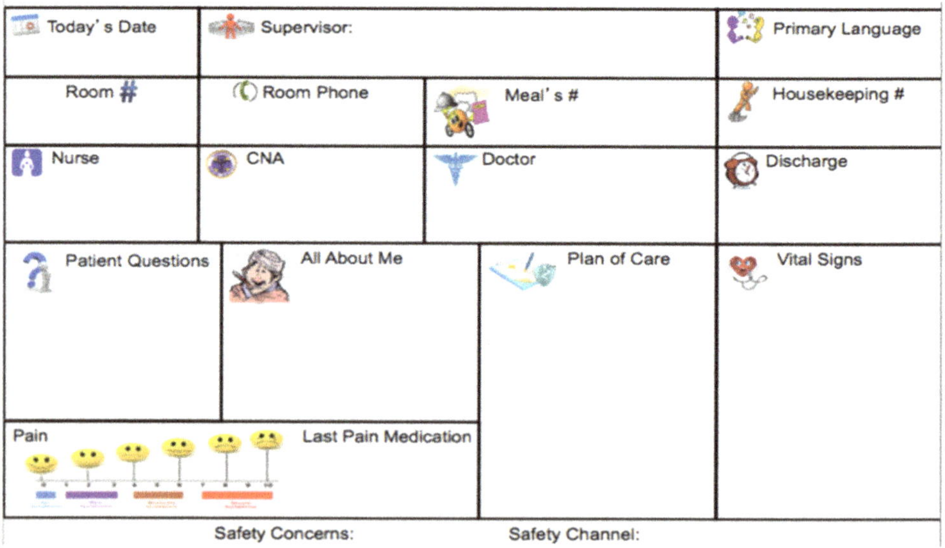

Figure 20

Information that is personally important to the patient can be captured in the All About Me section of the Whiteboard so anyone who enters the patient's room can glance at interesting facts about the patient and use that information to make a personal connection. Examples of information I have seen reflected here are hobbies, pet names, number of children and grandchildren, where they were born, favorite movie, food, book, and vacation destination. Listening and communicating carefully is critical in connecting with others because the personal connection we make with others sparks the best and lifts the moods of others.

Spark the Best and Lift the Mood of Others

For the purpose of this book, mood refers to the emotional state that impacts the quality of employee feelings. STAR performers elevate their own mood and the mood of others around them. They recognize that mood sets the tone that affects those they come in contact with throughout the day. A positive mood energizes a person, which promotes contagious enjoyment, optimism and fulfillment. Have you ever experienced someone who walks in the room and the mood immediately shifts – positive or negative. STAR Performers understand that their attitude and behavior either enriches the culture by lifting others up or squashes the culture by deflating the attitude and mood of others. To lift the mood of others, STAR Performers demonstrate enthusiasm, optimism, appreciation and seek possibilities.

Demonstrate enthusiasm, optimism and seek possibilities

STAR Performers appreciate that enthusiasm, optimism, appreciation and seeking possibilities creates infectious confidence and positivity. They are enthusiastic about living the purpose, delivering the promises and achieving the goals. Despite the reality of challenges and obstacles, they remain optimistic about the future and what can be accomplished. STAR Performers are not bound by existing paradigms that may inhibit their ability to see and seek new possibilities. A possibility mindset allows STAR Performers to identify opportunities during threats. They explore the question "what is impossible to do today but if it could be done would fundamentally change the way we do things that would lead to outstanding patient care, experience and safety?"

Stay focused on making the important things matter most

A distinctive trait of STAR Performers is their ability to stay focused on what matters most – the strategic agenda. Chasing the fad of the day does not distract them. They are incredibly disciplined on what matters most and ensure that everything aligns to what is most important. This focus allows them to minimize activities that do not contribute to the agenda, which abates pursuing too many things at that same time. They know that initiative overload leads to demand exceeding capacity, which drains energy, focus and time that could otherwise be spent on the most critical items. STAR Performers know what really matters and this is where they place their attention, time and energy. For an organization what matters most are its purpose, promise, vision, goals and core values. Leaders know that when these matter most, profitability will follow. But when they make profitability matter most, they will consistently deviate eroding their ability to deliver on what matters most.

Build trust and social capital through high quality relationships

STAR Performers know they cannot be successful in seclusion from others and they recognize that the quality of life at work is shaped by how well they relate to others and well others relate to them. Trust is the foundation to productive and high performing relationships. STAR Performers are trusted for 1) doing the right things, 2) being competent in their job skills and knowledge, and 3) truly caring about the success of others. High quality relationships are also influenced by the previously mentioned characteristics – caring deeply, connecting genuinely, sparking the best and lifting the moods of others, being enthusiastic, optimistic, possibility seeking, and staying focused on what matters most.

Provide Solutions

STAR Performers do not lament over a problem but rather work toward finding solutions. They understand that focusing too much on a problem generates fear, anxiety and powerlessness whereas focusing on solutions creates optimism, hope and empowerment. Problems, issues and challenges do exist but to be problem or solution focused is a choice. With a problem orientation, people are stuck in the present and are unable to move forward while solution-orientated people provide a means for moving forward, seeing possibilities and achieving next level performance. STAR Performers see a problem and have a desire to understand it, the causes, and quickly move to discovering a solution that fixes the problems. Conversely, problem oriented people take ownership of problem identification but offer no viable solutions for addressing the problem. Please don't misunderstand; problem identification is necessary to uncover innovative solutions. STAR Performers focus on identifying problems related to performance tied to advancing the purpose, promise, vision, goals and core values and they are quick to offer solutions to further advance the achievements needed to advance the strategic agenda of the organization.

Respond to adversity with resilience

Adversity occurs on a daily basis and it comes in many shapes, sizes and degrees. STAR Performers work to increase their capacity and effectiveness in responding to difficult of challenging circumstances. Peak Learning, Inc. has two wonderful tools, one for assessing one's Adversity Quotient (AQ) and another for determining one's Grit. Basically, people with higher grit respond better to adversity, which leads to better results. Using the STAR formula once again, an adversity situation occurs, a productive or unproductive thought about the situation is produced, an action happens, and a result ensues. The STAR Performer is aware of their AQ and Grit and developed their capacity to better deal with adversity.

What are woodpeckers and how do you detect them?

The performance of any department or organization is nothing more or less than the collective performance of the people. This is because it is people who make decisions, take action and behave with others. In other words, people determine the results of the organization. This is why never compromising on having the right people in the right jobs at the right time doing the right things matters. People performance is a influenced by of the following four factors:

1. Performance Level: High, Middle, Low
2. Talent Level: A, B, C, D
3. Engagement Level: Engaged, Disengaged, Actively Disengaged
4. Change Level: Design, Default, Defiance

The reality is that organizations contain high, middle, and low performers ranging in talent from A players, B players, C players, and D players. All too often, leaders are unwilling or ill-equipped to deal with low performers or to manage and match the talent level to the complexity of the role. In other words, the bandwidth of an individual should be considered when appointing them to a given role, particularly when role is difficult. As an example, it is imprudent to assign a C-level player to a highly complex function. Highly complex roles demand that A-Level Talent be assigned to them.

Additionally, the factor of engagement plays a role in performance. A number of studies have shown that the percentage of disengaged and actively disengaged employees outnumber those who are engaged or fully engaged. In fact, the Gallup Organization in their State of the Global Workplace Report [20] report that only 30% of the U.S. workforce is engaged in their work and that actively disengaged employees costs the U.S. between $450 billion and $550 billion per year.

Finally, how people react to change impacts their contribution to the enterprise. Figure 21 displays the 20-50-30 Rule in change management where 20% of employees are in change by design. Meaning when change is introduced, these employees are early adopters and change agents. Roughly 50% are in change by default meaning they take a wait and see approach. The bottom 30% are in change by defiance meaning they act out in ways that prevent the change from taking hold.

Figure 21

To ensure that the organization is being staffed with high performing people the performance level, talent level, engagement level and change level need to be understood and addressed.

Now, there is special group of people in change by defiance that cannot be ignored. It has been estimated that this toxic group of people can range from 3% to 6% of the workforce, and if left unchecked, can create enormous disruption and destruction over time as illustrated in Figure 22.

Figure 22

The Ark represents a department or organization, the animals symbolize the employees and Noah is the leader. Noah is frantically trying to catch one animal, the woodpecker, which is creating enormous destruction to the Ark. Once caught, Noah will try to rehabilitate the woodpecker trying to change its true nature. Unfortunately, you cannot rehabilitate a woodpecker. The best course of action is to help the woodpecker find his happiness somewhere else. This, of course, begs the question, how does one detect a woodpecker? There are three key questions that will distinguish a woodpecker from others in the change by defiance category. The three questions are:

1. Knowing what you know now, would you hire this person again?
2. If the person resigned, would you rejoice?
3. Would the team rather work short staffed than to work this individual?

If you answer "No", "Yes", and "Yes" to the three questions above, you might just have a woodpecker.

Not dealing with woodpeckers damages your credibility as a leader, especially with your high performers. It is incumbent to identify and rid yourself of woodpeckers because they are damaging the ability to live the purpose, delivery promises, achieve the vision, accomplish the goals and embody the core values.

What are the people practices that influence employee performance and how to transform them to achieve cultural excellence?

Over the years I have noticed a number of people practices that lead to higher levels of performance. The principle challenge I have observed is the lack of rigor and discipline by leaders needed to create and sustain the proven practices. There is tendency to relax and drift into an autopilot mentality.

The most critical function of a leader, as mentioned earlier, is to find, recognize and secure the future for their area of responsibility. To accomplish this primary role and to avoid drifting into autopilot related to people practices, leaders must embrace that one of their critical functions is to staff their department and organization with high performing people where high performance is a combination of employees' performance, engagement, talent levels and their change readiness. There are any number of methods that that leaders can use to influence how long an employee will stay and how productive they are in an organization including the following:

1. Leadership Style
2. Hiring Practices
3. Appointment Strategies
4. Lines of Sight
5. Accountability Standards
6. Training, Education and Career Development
7. Career Development
8. Recognition and Rewards
9. Personal Ownership
10. Signals

Leadership Style

The leader's style has a profound impact on the performance of their people. Consider this, a leader fosters a culture that influences behavior that produces results. In other words, results are driven by peoples' behavior, peoples' behavior is influenced by the culture and the culture is created by the way a leader leads.

Intended or unintended, the majority of leaders I have observed use a style that creates a negative tone in the culture. Ben Zander refers to this as the Downward Spiral, which basically proposes that in any given day the percentage of negative messages significantly outweighs positive messages in departments and organizations. If you doubt my observation, I invite you to listen carefully to the messages being sent and the way they are being delivered in your organization. Ask yourself, did the messages I hear today and the way in which they were conveyed make feel good or bad about my workday? Better yet, ask yourself, did the messages I delivered today and the way in which I conveyed them make my employees feel good or bad about their workday?

Joel Barker [21] offered one of my favorite definitions of a leader needed in the 21st century that has particular relevance for leadership style. The definition is "*a leader is someone you follow to a place you wouldn't go to by yourself.*" In the context of leadership style, it is intuitive that followers will be much more engaged, energized and connected with leaders who are optimistic, enthusiastic, smart, flexible, open-minded, caring, appreciative, happy, supportive and emotionally intelligent.

This does not mean they don't have high standards, because they do. It also doesn't mean they aren't tough or hold people accountable. It means they recognize, expect and trigger the best in their employees. A leader who needs employees to follow them to a place they wouldn't go to by themselves needs people to act out of commitment, not compliance. Compliance comes from a place of fear where commitment comes from a place of hope, confidence and caring.

A leader must live and conduct themself in a way that people choose to follow them to a place they wouldn't go to by themselves. Of course this begs the question, where is this place? The place is living the purpose, delivering the promise, achieving the vision, accomplishing the goals and embodying the core values. In other words, the place is building a bridge from the current state to the future state as outlined in the strategic plan.

The power of a leader's style was highlighted in Joel Barker's Leadershift video [22] where he cited Professor Tor Dahl from the University of Minnesota. Professor Tor Dahl found that changes in a leaders style could improve the productivity of followers by more than ten times. The study focused on how a leader exerted control, positive or negative; what kind of stress they engaged, positive or negative; and how satisfied or dissatisfied the employee was with their work. Leaders with a positive style created excitement, established challenging goals, were enthusiastic, fostered a rich work environment, shared decision-making, provided resources and constantly expected the best. By contrast, leaders with a negative style used negative controls such as threats, condemnation, fear, rejection and scornful behaviors. The ultimate conclusion is that over the long-term, there was no way a negative leader could ever compete with a positive leader in terms of loyalty, commitment and productivity.

Figure 23 is a simple and yet useful exercise in identifying behaviors to start, stop and continue to improve the leaders style and how they impact the culture and engagement of their followers. The numerous research findings by the Gallup Organization on employee engagement clearly report that the most important contributor to employee engagement is the quality of their direct leader. Endeavor to abandon behaviors that don't work, continue behaviors that do and embrace new behaviors that will generate great followership and engagement.

Behaviors I need to Start	Behaviors I need to Stop	Behaviors I need to Continue

Figure 23

In addition to demonstrating a leadership style that sparks possibilities in others, leaders need to engage in uncompromising hiring practices and appointment strategies. Leaders also should develop department and individual Part-to-Plays, which feed the development of clear and appropriately weighted accountability standards. Training and education should be provided to ensure knowledge and skills sets needed to perform the job are current. An equal amount, if not more, of the education should focus on reinforcing living the purpose, delivering the promises and embodying the core values. Career development, rewards and recognition are factors influencing employee engagement as well and signals should be identified, assessed and aligned to the core values of the organization.

Hiring Practices

In my opinion, from years of observation, making the right hire is too often compromised for expediency. I believe one should never compromise on the hire, particularly for critical positions, especially leadership positions. Earlier, the following simple metaphor was used to describe the importance of being steadfast in hiring practices. If you need eagles, hire eagles, don't hire turkeys and expect them to soar like eagles. There is not enough training, motivation or coaching that will ever enable turkeys to soar like eagles. Additionally, the business case for making the right hire is examining the fully loaded cost of making a hiring mistake. It has been estimated that the cost of turnover can range from 1 to 6 times the annual salary depending on the position. In healthcare, the most recent studies estimate that the fully loaded cost for one physician leaving the organization is approximately $1 million.

The hiring process should begin by developing a Success Profile for the position. The Success Profile describes the essential and important competencies, knowledge and cultural attributes needed to be successful in the job. The essential and important competencies and knowledge will vary for each job but the cultural attributes should be the same regardless of the position. This is because everyone should live the purpose, deliver the promises, embody the core values and demonstrate the vital few behaviors related to each core value.

There are many instruments, techniques and simulations that can aid in determining the best candidate for the job. However, not enough attention is paid to ensuring the right cultural fit based on the purpose, promise, core values and crucial behaviors.
For determining the likelihood of success in a given position, TalentLift, led by a psychometric expert Chris Steilberg, is an organization that does an outstanding job of providing evidence-based instruments for determining the potential fit of candidates for a given position.

It is recommended to compliment the robust tools offered by TalentLift with an internal interview process. Figure 24 is a sample Behavior and Value-Based Interview Guide for a Chief Medical Officer position.

Interview Guide

Candidate Name	Interview Date:
Job Applied: Chief Medical Officer	Interviewer Name:

Interview Questions	Rating Scale 1 Does not meet expectations	 2 Meets expectations	 3 Exceeds expectations
1. Please tell me what has happened during the day at work when you go home feeling really good and feeling really bad. Notes:	☐	☐	☐
2. Please tell me how you have engaged and aligned physicians to something strategically or operationally important. Notes:	☐	☐	☐
3. Please tell me about dyad or triad relationships you have built. Notes:	☐	☐	☐
4. Please tell about what you believe about organizational culture? Notes:	☐	☐	☐
5. Please tell me what role you have played in fostering a patient centric culture. Notes:	☐	☐	☐
6. Please tell what you believe are the most important factors that drive a patient's experience from their perspective. Notes:	☐	☐	☐
7. Please tell me about what you believe about employee engagement. Notes:	☐	☐	☐
8. Please tell me how you have improved employee engagement. Notes:	☐	☐	☐
9. What was your last boss's name? Tell me about NAME. When I talk with NAME, what will he/she tell me your strengths and limitations? Notes:	☐	☐	☐
10. Please tell me what you are deeply passionate about at work. Notes:	☐	☐	☐
11. Please tell me about the most difficult change you had to lead. What made it difficult and what was the outcome? Notes:	☐	☐	☐
Overall Assessment *(Complete sections below at conclusion of interview)*			
Leadership Competence/Presence	☐	☐	☐
Compassionate Attitude	☐	☐	☐
Culture Aptitude	☐	☐	☐
Overall Assessment	☐	☐	☐

Recommended Decision: ☐ Hire ☐ Don't Hire

Figure 24

This Interview Guide was developed to explore the candidates' experiences with key related job duties and cultural qualities for a Chief Medical Officer position. The questions used in the Interview Guide were customized based on the requirements of the role along with determining the cultural fit of the candidate around compassion and a patient-centric orientation. A multidisciplinary interview team was assembled and trained on how to interview the candidates in one-on-one and team-based interviews using the Interview Guide. The interview training included how to probe for additional details after the candidate provided an answer to a given interview question. Once the interviews were completed, the team assembled to share their impressions and determine which candidate to hire or to determine if the process should continue until the absolute right person for the role was discovered.

Additionally, it can be very revealing to administer a simulation of a frequent situation or circumstance that the position encounters that will expose the likely behaviors that will be experienced from the candidate on the job. The hiring process is critical to selecting the right people that meet the job requirement capabilities and have the cultural virtues that align to the core values.

Appointment Strategies

Another common mistake is not matching the talent level with the complexity of the department or function, especially for leadership roles. Complexity refers to the degree of difficulty to manage and lead a function. The degree of difficulty can be influenced by the scope and pace of the work intensified by volume, acuity, staffing models and ratios, financial contribution and regulatory requirements. It is imperative that capacity of the leader be considered when appointing to a particular complex function.

How many times have you seen a high performing individual contributor be moved into a leadership role only to fail miserably? He's a great nurse so certainly he will be a great nurse leader. Or, she is a great pharmacist so naturally she will be a great pharmacy leader.

Practically speaking, it will be difficult to staff the organization with A-Level talent for every position. However, the goals should be to continuously upgrade the talent level at every opportunity. Organizations will have A, B, C, and D level talent when they begin the journey to purposefully manage their talent. Executives should determine the percentage of leaders in the organization that fall within each talent level. A careful analysis should then be completed to identify what percentage of A-Level talent is assigned to highly complex functions. Figure 25 displays a helpful tool for determining the Complexity of Function (CoF).

	Complexity of Function				
	Rating Scale				
	Never	Rarely	Sometimes	Freqently	Always
Assessment Statements	1	2	3	4	5
Leader has large span of control/responsible for a large number of people					
Function experiences high patient volumes					
Function responsible for contributing to the financial success of the organization					
Function is highly political					
Function is highly regulated					
Function has a matrixed organizational structure					
People in the function have to work at a fast pace					
Shelf life of key practices (technology/equipment/supplies) is short					
Evidence based medical practices change frequently					
Comlexity of patient condition is high requiring very specialized skills					

Figure 25

The factors that contribute to the complexity of the function include:

- Leader has large span of control/responsible for large number of people
- Function experiences high patient volumes
- Function responsible for contributing to the financial success of the organization
- Function is highly political
- Function is highly regulated
- Function has a matrix organizational structure
- People in the function have to work at a fast pace
- Shelf life of key practices is short
- Evidence based medical practices change frequently
- Complexity of patient condition is high requiring very specialized skills

The complexity of the function impacts the leader's ability to be successful. When a leader's talent capacity falls short of matching the level of complexity of the function then the odds for success are diminished. Therefore, the purpose of appointment practices is to match the talent level with the complexity of function to improve the leader's odds of success.

Part-to-Play

The Part-to-Play is a useful method to ensure that each function and every individual understands their specific role in helping achieve the strategic and operational goals of the organization. As an example, Figure 26 displays a completed Part-to-Play for the Human Resource function's and an HR employee's role in supporting the following four strategies of the organization.

1. Grow outpatient market share from 15% to 18% in 18 months
2. Move from a 3 star rating to a 4 star rating in HCAHPS in 18 months
3. Open a new rehabilitation hospital in the summer of 2019
4. Expand primary care services from 243 employed physicians to 363 employed physicians in 24 months

Human Resource Function

Organizational Goal	Department Contribution	My Contribution
Grow outpatient market share from 15% to 20% in 18 months.	1. Complete needs assessment to determine support needed from HR to support the growth target 2. Update HR plan to support staffing needs of growth target	a. Administer needs assessment and develop report outlining needed HR support
Move from a 3 star to a 4 star rating in HCAHPS in 18 months.	1. Provide education and training on patient experience improvement 2. Provide coaching to staff who interact with patients and family members 3. Assess and improve the culture of targeted departments	a. Design the patient experience improvement curriculum b. Administer a culture assessment and develop culture readiness report
Open the new Rehabilitation Hospital in the summer of 2019	1. Develop a workforce plan to staff the new hospital 2. Recruit, select and onboard the leadership team for the new hospital 3. Recruit, select, and onboard staff for the new hospital	a. Identify the staffing needs for the new hospital b. Source and recruit people to fill the staffing needs c. Provide candidates to hiring leader
Expand primary care services from 243 employed physicians to 363 employed physicians in 24 months	1. Develop total compensation model for new physicians 2. Develop the employment contract for new physicians 3. Onboard new physicians	a. Develop the employment contract and review and finalize with the Legal Department

Figure 26

Too often employees are unaware of how their work directly or indirectly contributes to the organization's strategic agenda. By using a Part-to-Play, it becomes clear how a function and how employees contribute to the success of strategic goals. The output of the individual's role in the Part-to-Play becomes the input for developing accountability standards.

Accountability Standards

Another useful people practice to influences employees' performance is the disciplined and appropriate use of accountability standards. Accountability

Standards reflect the work expectations including required job goals, duties and behaviors.

The job goals include specific targets that designate what is necessary to exceed, meet, or not meet expectations. The relevant goals for any position should be gleaned from the result of the Part-to-Play to ensure alignment to the organization's priorities. Each Accountability Standard should be weighted to convey the relative importance of the standard in relationship to the company's priorities. Of course, the weighting of the standard may change from year to year based on the needs of the business. An example of a Leadership Accountability Standard for financial performance of a non-revenue-producing department might be as follows:

Department Financial Performance: Achieve at or below department budget for the year. (Weight 10%)

- Exceeds Standard: 2.0% or more below budget
- Meets Standard: Equal to or up to 1.99% below budget
- Does Not Meet Standard: Over budget

A common mistake leaders make is to weight a standard inappropriately to the priorities that are being messaged. For example, senior leaders declare that the patient experience, including the quality of care is the most important priority for the organization and yet this standard is only weighted at 15% while other standards are weighted more. This approach leads to confusion, misalignment and people dedicating their focus, effort and time to the more heavily weighted standards.

Figure 27 provides an example of a completed Accountability Standards form where the following five priorities are reflected:

1. Patient Quality
2. Patient Experience
3. Employee Engagement
4. Department Finance
5. Essential Behaviors

Sample Accountability Standard Form

Employee Name:		Evaluator Name:	
Job Title:		Department:	

Patient Quality: Reduce SEPSIS Mortality Rate.	Weight	Evaluation	Performance
• Exceeds Standard: Below CMS National Benchmark • Meets Standard: At CMS National Benchmark • Does Not Meet Standard: Above CMS National Benchmark	25%	☐ Exceeds (1.0) ☐ Meets (.5) ☐ Does Not Meet (0)	
Patient Experience: Achieve HCAHPS top box score.	**Weight**	**Evaluation**	**Performance**
• Exceeds Standard: ≥ 85% top box score on RN communication • Meets Standard: Between 82% - 84% top box on RN communication • Does Not Meet Standard: Below 82% top box on RN communication	25%	☐ Exceeds (1.0) ☐ Meets (.5) ☐ Does Not Meet (0)	
Employee Engagement: Increase ratio of engaged to disengaged employees.	**Weight**	**Evaluation**	**Performance**
• Exceeds Standard: 40% engaged employees • Meets Standard: 35% - 39% engaged employees • Does Not Meet Standard: Below 35% engaged employees	20%	☐ Exceeds (1.0) ☐ Meets (.5) ☐ Does Not Meet (0)	
Department Finance: Achieve at or below department budget for the year.	**Weight**	**Evaluation**	**Performance**
• Exceeds Standard: 2.0% or more below budget • Meets Standard: Equal to or up to 1.99% below budget • Does Not Meet Standard: Over budget	10%	☐ Exceeds (1.0) ☐ Meets (.5) ☐ Does Not Meet (0)	
Essential Behaviors: Consistently demonstrates the essential behaviors.	**Weight**	**Evaluation**	**Performance**
• Makes eye contact, smiles, and greets the patient • Escorts patient and family members to their destination • Washes hands when entering and leaving a patient room • Makes a personal connection with the patient • Provide a gentle touch on the patient hand or shoulder	20%	☐ Exceeds (1.0) ☐ Meets (.5) ☐ Does Not Meet (0)	

Figure 27

The job duties reflect the core activities required of a given position. This could include preparing budgets, building relationships, preparing reports, conducting analyses, administering medications, performing surgeries, preparing food or repairing broken equipment - in other words, the job duties are the day-to-day requirements to carry out the job successfully.

The organization's purpose, promises and core values should be the drivers for determining the essential behaviors that are reflected in the Accountability Standards. If shifting the culture is vital then the behavioral standards should be weighted heavily to express the seriousness of demonstrating the needed behaviors. It is important to remember that behaviors are observable – things people do and say.

It is recommended that leaders conduct formal monthly one-on-one discussions with their direct reports to review progress and performance for each standard and to make corrective adjustments needed to be within the targeted ranges for meeting and exceeding expectations. A helpful guide in having monthly and annual performance discussions is depicted in Figure 28. The purpose of the monthly and annual performance review is to engage in a productive and collegial conversation about what is working and what needs to be enhanced to sustain and improve performance.

Before the Session	Opening the Session	During the Conversation	Closing the Session

• Prepare, Prepare, Prepare
• Review the scores that have been provided for each accountability standard
• Take time to think about your colleague and identify top culture/behavior & performance metric strengths *(individually & their impact on the metrics)*
• What are the opportunities for growth *(individually & their impact on the metrics)*
• Look at performance beyond the scores
• Identify supporting examples
• Ask your colleague what time works best for them to meet & schedule
	• Provide a warm greeting
	• Make a personal connection
	• Thank them for their time
	• Be the mirror & come from a place of compassion & appreciation
	• Share the value they bring to the team (culture/behavior/leadership perspective & performance metrics)
	• Explain the overall process
	  • Share why this is important
	  • Share this is a new process & a baseline
	  • Provide an overview of what will be discussed
	    • Review the performance evaluation & take a look at your current performance & how we are doing
	    • Discuss the strengths they bring as well as explore opportunities for individual growth & development
	    • Ask for ideas on how they believe they can improve
		• Think about their overall performance
		  • Culture & metrics
		• High performing in all areas
		  • Share how well they are doing
		  • Thank them for their contribution
		  • Ask for their commitment in spreading best practice
		  • Always begin with sharing what they are doing well
		  • Thank them for their contribution
		  • Share the areas of opportunity & ask what they make of it.
		  • Identify ideas for improvement & support needed. Together identify developmental goals
		  • Discuss where they may be struggling & need support.
		  • Seek out assistance by identifying how others can support them
			• Provide a warm closing
			• Thank them for their time
			• Let them know how much you appreciate them and their contribution
			• Ask them how you can support their efforts if needed
			• Let them know about any follow up
			  • Review developmental plan as needed

Figure 28

Training, Education and Career Development

It is obvious that developmental opportunities provided to employees and leaders should align and support the requirements of accomplishing the job duties, the strategic and operational requirements of the organization. For our purposes here, training refers to building the skills necessary to perform the job tasks proficiently, education denotes building knowledge and expanding mindsets, and career development provides people with career tracks that are suitable to their qualifications and capacity.

What is not so obvious is the importance of providing training, education, and career development that reinforces the needed culture. Training and education should also be provided to build skills sets, knowledge and shift mental models to support living the purpose, delivering promises and demonstrating the essential behaviors associated with the core values of the organization. During a culture transformation process, many people struggle to understand how to behave in a way that 1) supports enhancing the culture or 2) delivers an exceptional experience to co-workers and patients. In the absence of reinforcement through training and education, people will resort to what they have always been accustomed to doing.

For career development, the needed experiences to gain the knowledge and skills required to advance along a given career path is a well-known practice. In addition to having the requisite capabilities, the best candidates for career growth should be able to both achieve results and live the culture. Promoting or advancing people who deliver results but do it at the expense of culture is gross negligence to the overall health and fitness of the organization's culture and long-term success. The best candidates achieve results while contributing to improving the health and fitness of the company's culture.

It should be noted that for leadership development an emerging model for expanding a leader's strategic, systemic thinking, change leadership, stakeholder relationship development and conflict management capabilities is vertical learning. Barrett C. Brown in his white paper entitled *The Future of Leadership for Conscious Capitalism* [23] *references* that "vertical learning is the transformation of how a leader thinks, feels and makes sense of the world." He goes on to make the distinction between horizontal and vertical learning by stating that "while vertical learning focuses on the *how*, traditional learning – or horizontal learning targets *what* a leader knows. Horizontal learning represents the knowledge and skills we acquire while operating at the same level of cognitive, emotional and relational complexity. Horizontal learning enables us to gain knowledge and build functional skills. Vertical learning broadens our view and permanently heightens our awareness, making us both wiser and more caring." Leadership development models of the future should include both horizontal and vertical learning to build the type of leadership that will needed in the 21st century marketplace.

Recognition and Rewards

In The Carrot Principle [24], Adrian Gostick and Chester Elton highlight the power of recognition and appreciation. "In response to the question 'My organization recognizes excellence,' the organizations that scored in the lowest fourth overall had an average return on equity of 2.4 percent, whereas those that scored in the top fourth had an average return on equity of 8.7 percent." Other business outcomes such as employee satisfaction, retention and customer satisfaction were positively impacted as well based on how well and often a manager recognizes the contribution of employees.

Remember, when employees leave by choice, they rarely leave an organization but rather an ineffective boss. When asked, employees who leave will tell you the number one reason for their departure was a lack of appreciation from their direct supervisor. The appreciation employees' want has to do with feeling valued by their leader for their contributions and accomplishments. This is not about rewards, bonuses or perks but rather genuine compliments for a job well done.

Personal Ownership

Culture begins at an individual level. It has been said that organizational transformation begins with individual transformation. Employees must take ownership of their attitude, understand how they show up every day and acknowledge the type of influence they carry with their co-workers. Tom Rath and Donald Clifton describe how one's behavior has a profound impact on others in their book *How Full Is Your Bucket?* [25], They state that…

> "Each of us has an invisible bucket. It is constantly emptied or filled, depending on what others say or do to us. When our bucket is full, we feel great. When it is empty, we feel awful.
>
> Each of us also has an invisible dipper. When we use that dipper to fill other people's buckets – by saying or doing things to increase their positive emotions – we also fill our own bucket. But when we use that dipper to dip from other's buckets – by saying or doing things that decrease their positive emotions – we diminish them and ourselves.
>
> A full bucket gives us a positive outlook and renewed energy. Every drop in that bucket makes us stronger and more optimistic. But an empty bucket poisons our outlook, saps our energy and undermines our will. That's why every time someone dips from our bucket, it hurts us.
>
> So we face a choice every moment of every day: We can fill one another's buckets, or we can dip from them. It's an important choice – one that profoundly influences our relationships, productivity, health and happiness."

A big part, if not the biggest part, of contributing to an Awakened Organization is how employees elect to show up for patients, co-workers and the organization. Each employee should consider how many people take their cue from them and think about whether their actions deposit into others' buckets or deplete from them. Each employee should ponder the following questions:

1. What are events that occur to me that make me feel emotionally depleted at work?
2. What are events that occur to me that really energize me at work?
3. What interactions have I had the past 24 to 48 hours with co-workers where I depleted their bucket? What specifically did I do?
4. What interactions have I had the past 24 to 48 hours with co-worker where I made a deposit into their bucket? What specifically did I do?

Answers to these questions will give your employees insight into how they are choosing to show up and the signals they are sending and receiving in every moment of everyday.

Signals

In Chapter 4 the power of signals was introduced. As a reminder, appropriately aligned signals to the desired culture will empower, invigorate and link people to what is important to achieve the desired results or misaligned signals will disempower, disengage or disconnect people. The practices and signals take many forms, some obvious and others barely noticeable. The people practices outlined in this chapter serve as signals to the people in the organization as well as the ones covered in Build a Strategy Supportive Culture chapter. The style of leaders, hiring practices, appointment strategies, Part to Play, accountability standards, training, education, career development, recognition and rewards all send signals to employees about the relative importance of strategy execution, fostering a healthy and fit culture, living the purpose, and delivering on promises. Any inconsistency in the alignment of these practices sends messages to employees about what is truly important in the company and their behavior will be governed by the signals they receive.

Staffing the organization with high performing people is the third element of The Awakened Organizational Model where high performance includes both producing results and living the culture.

A high performing employee lives the purpose, delivers on the promises, embodies the values and fulfills their job duties. As a reminder, people need to be both technically and culturally elite. An individual who is technically elite performs their job duties at a high level. They have the knowledge, skills and abilities that are required of their particular job. To be culturally elite, people exemplify the behaviors reflected in the core values and they make others around them better by the way the show up through their attitude and actions.

The biggest mistakes that are frequently made is compromising on the hire and not adjusting signals. Hiring the right talent with the right cultural attributes is absolutely critical – never compromise on the hire, particularly for mission critical positions. Also, the signals being sent should be examined, re-imagined and altered to support the development of a healthy and fit culture.

Questions to Consider:

1. How often do we compromise on staffing the organization with high performing people and why?
2. How do we consider the complexity of a function when appointing talent?
3. Have we been deliberate in appointing A-Level talent to highly complex departments?
4. What hiring practices do we use to differentiate talent?
5. What would it be like in our organization if everyone mastered the STAR technique?
6. What is our Culture Quotient and what should we do to improve it?
7. How does our leadership style affect the mood of our people?
8. Do we know who the Woodpeckers are and are we willing to deal with them?

9. Have we analyzed and adjusted signals to align to the culture we are trying to create?
10. How well do our training, education, and career development reinforce the core values and essential behaviors?
11. What recognition practices do our leaders use to express sincere appreciation to our employees?

Chapter 6

Multiply the Efforts Through Continuous Process Improvement

"Funny how we don't have the time to improve, but we have plenty of time to perform work inefficiently and to resolve the same problems over and over."

W. Edward Deming

The intent of this chapter is not to repeat the excellent resources available on performance improvement techniques such as Lean Production, PDSA, PDCA, or Six Sigma but rather describe why so many process improvement efforts fall short of delivering the intended outcomes and the key success factors that will increase the odds of success with process optimization efforts.

Leaders in an Awakened Organization understand the linkage of process improvement to the achievement of business goals through greater efficiency and effectiveness. Processes are the activities performed by people in an organization whereby inputs (people, materials, capital, supplies, and equipment) are transformed into outputs (services and products) to achieve specific results. In other words, processes are what people do for the company.

A continuous process improvement mindset first addresses two fundamental questions. First, why do we do what we do? The answer to this question will determine if the set of work activities should be done in the first place. If there is a clear value added reason for doing what we do then the second question should be explored. Why do we do it the way we do it? This question requires a constant examination of the way work is performed and how a set of steps can be redesigned to improve cycle time, reduce costs, increase quality and deliver greater value to the ultimate customer of the process.

This chapter will address the key success factors needed to navigate the most common pitfalls of process improvement efforts. The key success factors are:

1. Ensure there is senior leader support in organizational alignment
2. Fix the processes that matter most
3. Be clear on and focus value for the ultimate customer of the process
4. Involve the right people
5. Keep it simple
6. View process improvement as a change initiative
7. Ensure that form follows function

Ensure there is senior leader support in Organizational Alignment

A key success factor in any process improvement effort is the level of support provided by senior leaders. In fact, the level of backing needed to redesign processes is the same for any change initiative. The executives need to be clear and specific about the vision for the effort by using vivid descriptions of what the world of work will look like, the picture, once the newly designed process is working as it is intended to work. Using vivid descriptions to describe the possibilities of the newly designed process will connect people at a feeling level, which ignites imagination and excitement about the future.

In addition to the well-defined picture, the executives need to articulate the why behind redesigning the process - the purpose or reason for changing the process should be explained. The reasons could include reducing costs, improving the patient experience, enhancing quality care, generating revenue, increasing market share, reducing harm or enabling the accomplishments of a strategic goal.

Next, the senior leaders need to communicate the plan for redesigning the process. In other words, the senior leaders need to describe the approach that will be used to analyze the existing process, identify shortcomings, design the ideal state and provide the needed resources to the initiative including assigning an executive champion to each process change for sponsorship, removing obstacles and providing the necessary resources.

The part to play is the next key component that senior leaders need to articulate. This includes describing what is needed from people impacted by the process redesign, how key stakeholders will benefit from the change and what support will be provided to help with the transition from the current to future state. Senior leaders should also describe the prize/penalty aspects of the redesign. The prize portion outlines the benefits that will be realized when success is achieved while the penalty piece describe the downside of not being successful. Figure 29 is the 5P Worksheet, which can be helpful when structuring key messages about the process change effort.

The change to be managed:	Insert here

5 Ps	What Will I Communication for This Change
1. Purpose • The reason for the change. Why does this need to happen? • What is the problem? What is the evidence to support the problem? • What would occur if no one acts to solve it?	
2. Picture • The vivid description of the desired state • What will the outcome look like? • How will it feel to be a participant in the outcome? • What is the What's In It For Me (WIIFM) for staff?	
3. Plan • What is the plan to get from here to there? • What is the timeline? What are the goals? • What are the key steps?	
4. Part to Play • My role – my responsibilities • How do I fit into this scheme? • What is my role? • How will my job change?	
5. Prize/Penalty • Describe the consequences • What is the upside of the change? • What is the downside of the change?	

Figure 29

To summarize, the 5Ps are:

- **Picture**: The vision for the process improvement.
- **Purpose**: The reason for embarking on the change.
- **Plan**: The approach that will be used to bring about the change.
- **Part to Play**: The responsibilities and accountabilities for those impacted by the change.
- **Prize/Penalty**: The upside of being successful and the downside of not being successful.

Another important role that senior leaders can play is to ensure that the people in the organization are not overwhelmed by initiative overload. It will be tempting to address as many of the failure points as possible at the same time. It is recommended that this temptation be resisted. Instead, ensure that process improvements are aligned to what matters most.

Fix the Processes that Matter Most

Senior leaders need to reject becoming distracted by everything that comes their way and focus their attention, time, and energy on what really matters most. This means being intentional rather than accidental or situational about the process improvement efforts to be undertaken.

> What really matters most is aligned to the strategic agenda of the organization – its purpose, vision, goals and strategies. Enlightened leaders understand that if these factors matter most, profitability will follow. But if they make profitability matter most, they will consistently erode their ability to be strategically successful. In other words, the senior leaders need to be on a mission and stay focused on improving the Strategy Critical Processes (SCPs), which could be the biggest culprits to people performing work in the most effective and efficient manner as possible.

In the busy and noisy world of day-to-day operations, it becomes easy for priorities to be distorted, which distracts people from improving processes related to what matters most. Senior leaders need to have the focus to cut through the clutter and prioritize process improvements that will yield the greatest desired outcomes. The following questions can be useful in determining which processes matter most.

1. What are our most important goals?
2. Which processes are barriers to goal achievement?
3. What are the consequences (positive and negative) of addressing the SCPs?

An additional perspective that will influence what matters most is accounting for whom the ultimate customer is of the processes being targeted for improvement.

To illustrate the need to focus on what matters most, I am reminded of a recent patient experience event with my father-in-law, Bob. Bob is a compassionate, gentle, kind soul who has loved his family unconditionally. Not long ago my wife and her sister shared that they have concerns about their father's declining health. Most recently, he had an acute illness where we thought we were going to lose him unnecessarily.

The onset of Bob's illness began on a Saturday evening around 7:30 p.m. My wife's sister visited him after her mother expressed concerns about Bob not feeling well. My sister-in-law called my wife who is a Registered Nurse to share his symptoms. My wife asked her to immediately call 911. The EMS team responded immediately and was prompt, thorough and quickly transported him to the nearest hospital.

When my wife arrived at the Emergency Department she noted that her Dad was struggling to breath, had an extremely rapid irregular heart rate, a wet cough and fluid in his legs and abdomen. The nurse assigned to Bob was courteous and very attentive. Per orders written by the Emergency Department physician the nurse administered a dose of IV medication to reduce the rapid heart rate, which had minimal effect. She also applied oxygen via a nasal cannula and ensured a chest x-ray was performed. The results of the chest x-ray confirmed a new diagnosis of Congestive Heart Failure. At this point in the process, the Emergency Department physician decided to admit Bob to a medical surgical unit and his care was transitioned to an Inpatient Hospitalist.

Throughout the next long 4 hours my wife and her sister witnessed an absolute neglect in care and a rapid decline of their Dad. His breathing was extremely labored and his heart rate continued to beat at a very fast rate. His nurse had made several attempts to contact the Inpatient Hospitalist for him to come to the Emergency Department, assess Bob and provide the necessary orders to continue the much-needed care. It was apparent she was just as frustrated as my wife with the significant delay in care. She even attempted to contact her supervisor to expedite the process. My wife was providing me with frequent updates as I sat in the waiting room and I remember her sharing she could see the Emergency Department physician sitting across from the hallway working on his computer. Both his assigned nurse and my wife knew that Bob was not receiving the proper care. The following are the observations about the experience:

- Minimal support was being provided to support his respiratory distress
- No additional medication was administered to reduce his rapid heart rate
- Medication was not administered to reduce the fluid overload he was experiencing in his body
- There was no ongoing assessment or care from the Emergency Department physician
- The hospitalist did not respond to the request to see Bob
- The nurse was trying to do her very best but she was constrained by the processes
- There was no expressed concern for Bob
- Several attempts were made to either have the Emergency Department physician continue to attend to Bob or obtain the necessary orders from the Hospitalist

At 12:30 a.m., my wife came out to the waiting room to provide an update and she said she thought we are going to have to call 911 to get her Dad out of here. After our conversation, she went back into see her father and found that he was beginning to turn blue. At this point she informed me about Bob's status and I decided to contact the CEO of the hospital to get immediate help. My wife walked over to the Emergency Department physician and said, "I need you to get up and immediately attend to my Dad or we are going to lose him". After the CEO was contacted, suddenly all the resources were available. The ICU team quickly arrived to care for Bob, the Emergency Department physician came into the room and stated "thank you for calling me in here". The much-needed support was provided for his respiratory status, more medication was administered to reduce his heart rate and a decision was made to transfer him to the Intensive Care Unit.

Rightfully or wrongfully, the experience in the Emergency Department shaped my family's perception of the rest of the care he would likely receive. Thankfully Bob recovered, was discharged and is doing well. When we think about the possibility of what could have happened to Bob, it weighs on our hearts, and we wonder how our work in healthcare can at times be so broken to the point where patient care and safety are in jeopardy. Clearly the handoff between physicians is a process that failed in this instance and it prevented them from actually seeing what was happening right before their very eyes.

The impact on outcomes in this situation was very apparent. Not only was the experience far from what healthcare systems strive to achieve, the broken processes led to an admission to the Intensive Care Unit as opposed to a Medical Surgical unit and an unnecessary increased length of stay.

This experience clearly contrasts a hospital that is first and foremost business and operationally centered versus one that truly embraces patient and family centeredness. The processes that mattered most at this hospital put the patient at risk. In healthcare, the processes that matter most should always be centered on what is best for the patient.

Ironically, the cost would have been significantly less if they had been patient centered. For example, an avoidable ICU admission, shortened stay if INR was addressed, not to mention lost revenue and what it will cost in word of mouth about the experience for this particular hospital.

Be clear on and focus value for the ultimate customer of the process

One of the biggest mistakes in process optimization work is not being clear about who the ultimate customer is of the process. In healthcare, it is tempting to believe that the patient is the ultimate customer of every process – this is not the case. Consider the ultimate customer as the end user of a given process.

The end user is the primary recipient of and dependent upon the quality of the outputs of the process, which serves as inputs for them to be able to perform their process to the expectation and standards of their ultimate customer. For example, the ultimate customer of a treatment plan is the patient. However, the physician relies on the output of others to be able to develop and implement the most effective treatment plan. The physician may depend on laboratory, radiology and other testing results to make the most effective treatment decisions. In this example, radiology and laboratory should view

the physician as the ultimate customer and design their processes to meet and exceed the expectations of the physician.
In Lean Production for example, we know that every process consists of value-add activities, value-enabling activities, non-value add required activities and non-value activities where value-add meets the following conditions:

1. The ultimate customer is willing to pay for it
2. The work is done right the first time
3. The work changes the service in a positive manner

Going back to our laboratory and radiology example, what does the physician experience from these two testing functions that 1) he/she would be unwilling to pay for, 2) work needed by the physician is not done right the first time, and 3) the work of the suppliers (radiology and laboratory) does not change the service to the physician in some positive manner. In other words, what are the breakdowns that prevent the physician from receiving the best output from radiology and laboratory in order to do their job for the patient? Ideally, radiology and laboratory would view physicians as their ultimate customer and seek to understand and meet the expectations of the end user of their services – the physicians.
For each SCP, the ultimate customer should be identified, and their expectations uncovered. The right people should then be enlisted to redesign the processes to meet and exceed the expectations of the ultimate customer.

Involve the right people

People support best what they help create. Unfortunately, all too often, consultants (internal and external) are used to analyze data, map existing processes, identify bottlenecks and redesign processes without involving those closest to the work. This approach is perceived by staff as expert advisors imposing practices, which leads to resistance, cynicism, reduced engagement and lower performance.

It is important to engage representatives that impact the performance of a given process from the initiating event that begins the process to the terminating activity, which ends the process. Also, anyone who provides valuable input into the process should be included. In other words, those closest to and involved in the process should be enlisted to map and redesign the process. This is important for several any reasons.

First, the staff's perception that processes are designed in a way that allows them to do their best work every day and they have input on how work is designed is a key driver of employee engagement. Next, people want a say in how their work is redesigned. They want to feel that their opinions and expertise are valued and appreciated. Third, people closest to the work know what works and what does not work. The employees clearly understand what frustrates them about their work and they are eager to be asked how to improve their world of work. Fourth, employees know how to fix the problems. When solutions are forced upon people they push back and feel insulted that they were not asked to provide ideas for improving their work. Finally, when involved, the staff will believe leadership cares about them, which will in turn lead to higher levels of engagement. According to a Modern Survey Report on The State of Employee Engagement, one of the key drivers of engagement is "My work gives me a feeling of personal accomplishment." When processes are encumbered by waste and bottlenecks it is difficult for employees to feel a sense of personal accomplishment or satisfaction.

I recall a particular example of the benefit of involving the right people in redesigning processes. The hospital was beleaguered with long-standing challenges and morale was at an all-time low. A number of consultants had been involved in helping address some of the key process issues in Surgical Services. As is often the case, these consultants did their assessment and made recommendations based on their particular playbook without involving the people the improvements would benefit. The improvements were rejected, morale plummeted, confidence in leaders eroded and the inefficiencies mounted.

When we were invited in, we immediately assembled a team of employees closest to the work. At the time, the staff was expectedly skeptical because of past efforts failing and not being included in the improvement efforts. Everything we did involve the staff, surgeons, and anesthesiologists – everyone that touched the process. They mapped the existing process, identified failure points, prioritized the issues, developed, owned and implemented the small tests of change plans. What were the end results?

The targets for each priority were exceeded; the staff was re-energized because they felt they were given a seat at the table and that their opinions mattered; STAR performers emerged, Woodpeckers revealed themselves and confidence in leadership lifted. As one staff member stated, "finally, someone cared enough to involve us and listen to our ideas."

This approach of involving the right people has proven successful in a number of process improvement efforts. In addition to involving the people closest to the work, it is important to also keep it as simple as possible.

Keep It Simple

In addition to involving the people closest to the work, the approach needs to be as simple as possible. All too often, complex methods are used which tends to overwhelm, alienate, and confuse those participating in the process improvement initiative. Now, it is important not to confuse simple with easy.

Simple and easy are often used interchangeably, and in many cases they are. But simple and easy are different words with different meanings. What is simple is not always easy. This is an important distinction, because we often look for so-called "silver-bullet" solutions to complex problems. We often fail to take into account that just because it is simple in theory does not mean it will be easy in practice. To illustrate the point, consider weight loss. Losing weight is simple in theory. You must create a negative calorie balance, meaning you must spend more energy than you consume. It really is that simple. Despite the simplicity, losing weight is one of the hardest things to do. Every day, thousands of people go on a diet only to be off it in a couple of weeks.

For process improvement, simple tools can be used to uncover, prioritize and address issues. However, consistently changing the way the work is carried out can be heavy lifting, particularly when addressing entrenched and difficult issues. A proven approach to combat this is to use small tests of change. A small test of change focuses on a particular problem with a reduced scope. According to the Institute for Healthcare Improvement, "a team learns from the test, what worked and what did not work? What should be kept, changed or abandoned? And uses the new knowledge to plan the next test. The team continues linking tests in this way, refining the change until it is ready for broader implementation." It should also be noted that people are far more willing to test a change when they know that changes can and will be modified as needed. Linking small tests of change helps overcome an organization's natural resistance to change and ensures stakeholder buy-in. Other benefits of using small tests of change include:

1. Increasing people's belief that the change will result in improvement.
2. Deciding which of several proposed changes will lead to the desired improvement.
3. Evaluating how much improvement can be expected from the change.
4. Deciding whether the proposed change will work in the actual environment of interest.
5. Determining which combinations of changes will have the desired effects on the important measures.
6. Assessing the costs, social impact and side effects from a proposed change.
7. Minimizing resistance upon implementation.

The reason to use small tests of change is to determine whether an idea could result in sustainable improvement. Changes can be tested under multiple conditions and with a variety of staff before being scaled. In other words, once the tests are completed and proven to be successful then the improvement can be expanded and spread in larger ways.

Just like the diet example, process improvement requires a change in practice and behavior, which can be the hardest part of the improvement effort. Involving people closest to the work and using small tests of change can aid in hardwiring sustainable change. Additionally, process improvement should be viewed as a change initiative requiring change management practices to identify and enlist key stakeholders.

View Process Improvement as a Change Initiative

Never underestimate the importance of employees' acceptance of change otherwise resistance will win the day. Process improvement efforts are themselves change initiatives that must include change management methods to minimize resistance and create an environment of change readiness.

According to various independent research studies, 60% to 90% of change initiatives fail because leaders focus solely on the quality of a proposed solution and not on engaging key stakeholders. A helpful formula to illustrate the power of combining a great solution with strong commitment is the equation S x C = IP, it's the quality of the proposed Solution (S) multiplied by the degree of stakeholder Commitment (C) in implementing that solution that determines Improved Performance (IP). Great process solutions alone are not enough to facilitate lasting change because at the end of the day it is people who perform.

When undertaking a process improvement project, successful leaders identify key stakeholders and stakeholder groups; assess their current and desired level of support, and determine how critical their support is to the success of the process improvement. Leaders also gather intelligence about the key stakeholders who are critical to the effort but currently don't support the initiative. Stakeholder intelligence includes understanding the stakeholder interests; needs, concerns and paradigms. It also includes determining what the stakeholders deeply care about and what assumptions they have about the process and improvement effort. With this stakeholder intelligence, messaging and influence strategies can be used to align the purpose of the process improvement to something that is important to the stakeholder.

Ensure that Form Follows Function

Poorly conceived organizational structures can dramatically affect the effectiveness and efficiency of processes. Complex and ill-conceived structures will lead to more process challenges because of silo thinking, unnecessary handoffs, bottlenecks and multiple leaders competing for control.

According to Lex Sisney, in The 5 Classic Mistakes in Organizational Structure: Or, How to Design Your Organization the Right Way [26], if the organization has a flawed design, it simply won't perform well. It must be structured (or restructured) to create a design that supports its function or business strategy." Lex goes on to say, "the functions an organization performs are the core areas or activities it must engage in to accomplish its strategy. The location of each function is where it is placed in the organizational structure and how it interacts with other functions. The authority of a function refers to its ability to make decisions within its domain and to perform its activities without unnecessary encumbrance."

If the structure does not account for the functions, location and authority then the workflow inefficiencies will be built into the organization leading to process challenges and breakdowns. For example, in one healthcare system it was not uncommon to have ten touch-points to be able to get something approved or accomplished.

The forth element of The Awakened Organizational Model, multiply their efforts through continuous process improvement is vital to improving performance and achieving the strategic priorities of the organization. This is because processes are the way work is organized and performed. Well-designed processes allow people to perform their duties unfettered by obstacles leading to improvements in quality, cost, productivity and cycle-times, which ultimately lead to shaping the experience of the patient.

Questions to Consider:

1. How does senior leadership need to show up differently to ensure process improvement success?
2. What are the processes that matter most in our organization that need to be improved?
3. Who are the ultimate customers of the processes that matter most?
4. Who are the right people to involve in the process improvement efforts?
5. How do we keep the approach simple enough for people to understand and relevant enough to scale once successful?
6. What change management approach will be used to ensure key stakeholders accept and buy-in to the process change?
7. How does the current structure of the organization help and hinder optimum process performance?

Chapter 7

Summary and Conclusion

"Imagination is more important than knowledge. Knowledge is limited. Imagination encircles the world."

Albert Einstein

I opened the book by suggesting that you imagine a world in healthcare where everyone is contributing their full potential self; a world where everyone is engaged and energized because they feel a special connection to the purpose of the organization; a world full of people partnering in the service of others. Let us take this a step further.

Imagine in your company that everyone understands and is committed to the direction of the your organization; you have a strategy supportive culture where everyone embodies the core values and demonstrates the essential behaviors; departments are staffed with high performing people; and continuous process improvement is being pursued for the processes that mattered most. If this were taking place you truly would have created an Awakened Organization.

Awakening Your Organization reflects the desire to awaken leaders to what is necessary to unlock the unlimited potential and possibilities for healthcare organizations through the synchronization of strategy, culture, people, and processes. An Awakened Organization is filled with people of who are optimistic, passionate, compassionate, energized, results oriented and engaged by a powerful culture that elicits the very best in others. Where a profoundly positive environment suffocates toxic and divisive behaviors and an agenda for what is best for the organization is followed.

Experience demonstrates that many organizations are likely to look for one hit wonders or silver bullets to achieve organizational performance excellence. At the same time, others will overcomplicate what's required to accelerate performance. The approach recommended within these chapters is based on practical experience and designed to be relatively simple and straightforward. Whether you are a small Critical Access Hospital or a large health system, the principles are the same; it's only the scope that changes. In summary, let's briefly review the primary Lessons and the Call to Action related to each.

Lesson 1: One of the most important roles of a leader is to spend time investigating and thinking about the future. This is as true for senior leaders as it is for leaders of service lines and other key functions. The purpose of spending time in the future is to develop an understanding about the potential emerging trends and paradigm shifts that could impact healthcare in the future. The emerging trends could be financial, clinical care models, competition, regulation, changing demographics, new technologies or other innovations. Spending time in the future allows a leader to find, recognize and secure the future by pursuing attractive opportunities and mitigating risks.

Call to Action: Set aside time reading, networking and attending conferences that provide a lens into where healthcare may be headed in the future and to expect the same from leaders of key service lines and other key corporate functions including but not limited to human resources, information technology, ancillary services and consumer expectations just to name a few.

Lesson 2: Armed with the intelligence gathered by spending time in the future, the strategic planning outlines what must be done to win in the market place. The Strategic Planning System includes assessing current and end states, developing goals and strategies, aligning strategic priorities to various leaders and functions, executing the strategies and continuously assessing and making corrective adjustments to unanticipated changes in market conditions.
Call to Action: Provide answers the following key questions:

1. What is our reason for being?
2. What are the primary current and future market conditions?
3. What are the opportunities and threats related to the current and future market conditions?
4. What is the main thing we would like to accomplish in the future?
5. What are our goals as expressed from A to B by When?
6. What are the strategies that will allow us to achieve each of the goals?

7. What are our promises to our patients and to our employees?
8. What does everyone need to believe for us to be successful?
9. What matters most right now?

Lesson 4: Culture matters because it is the great amplifier of performance. Remember, culture is evidenced by what others experience from our organization – patients, family members and employees. A healthy and fit culture is the collective behavior of people in the organization shaped by deeply shared beliefs aligned to the purpose, promise, vision and goals, strengthened by belief-reinforcing signals and evidenced by incredible memorable experiences of employees, patients and family members. By contrast, an unhealthy and unfit culture is the collective behavior of people in the organization shaped by various beliefs misaligned to organizational priorities, reinforced by conflicting signals and evidenced by a variety of experiences for employees, patients and family members ranging from positively memorable to positively terrible. So, if you want to know how healthy and fit your culture is, look to the experience your employees and patients have with your organization. Your Culture Quotient, built from the organization's core beliefs and vital behaviors, will inform you about the overall health and fitness of your culture. To transform the culture you have to 1) define the desired culture, 2) assess and design cultural practices and behaviors, 3) implement programmatic culture change, and 4) monitor progress and adjust as needed.

Call to Action: Be serious about culture. First determine the core beliefs that everyone must embody to live the purpose, deliver on the promise, achieve the vision and accomplish the goals. Then, develop the essential core values from the core beliefs. For each core value, express the vital behaviors that everyone must demonstrate, always. Next, ensure signals are aligned to reinforce the desired culture.

Lesson 5: If culture is the great amplifier of performance then people are the great amplifier of culture. Culture is what others experience from the people in your organization from their behavior. So, hiring, appointing, keeping and developing the right people is central to the organization's success.

Call to Action: Never compromise on people and build people practices that allow you to find, hire, appoint, retain and develop people that match your exacting standards as expressed by what is required both technically and culturally. Match the bandwidth of the talent, particularly leadership, with the complexity of the role and/or department. Identify and deal with Woodpeckers. Strengthen how leaders lead so they inspire the best from others and build everyone's ability to use the STAR formula.

Lesson 6: Leaders in an Awakened Organization understand the linkage of process improvement to the achievement of business goals through greater efficiency and effectiveness of essential processes. There are a number of factors that influence how processes evolve over time to include waste, bottlenecks and errors, which create hassle factors for people performing the work and frustration for the customers of the work output.

Call to Action: Ensure senior leaders appropriately support the process improvement priorities. Focus on fixing the processes that matter most and be clear on who the ultimate customer of the process is. Be sure to involve the right people; the people closest to the work should help map the existing process, identify failure points, redesign the process, and participate in the implementation of the process improvement plan. Keep it simple by starting with a reasonable scope by embracing a small test of change and then scale as appropriate. Use change management techniques in the process improvement effort to gain stakeholder commitment. Finally, be aware that complexity in structure can lead to significant process performance issues.

I began this book with a story about my dad that profoundly impacted me and ignited a flame within to help transform healthcare to be strategically focused, culturally elite, staffed with high performing people and continuously focused on process improvement. While there are several examples of high performing hospitals and health systems throughout our nation, we still have a long ways to go, particularly in becoming truly patient-centric.

My bias and aspiration is that every patient, despite their clinical condition, will receive high quality, compassionate and safe care like Nicole provided for our dear friend's husband. For those who have been and are on this journey to revolutionize and re-humanize healthcare, I offer you this message from *The Heart of a Caregiver* [27].

"*Most of us at some point in our lives experience what it's like to be a Caregiver for a limited time...caring for a small child or a family member who is either sick or is recovering from an accident or surgery, or helping with the care of an aging or disabled loved one. During such times we begin to understand the physical demands and emotional strains related to the constant care of another individual. It helps us gain valuable insight into the level of patience, compassion and dedication required from the special people who make the choice to commit their lives in service to those who are hurting, to those who need comfort and encouragement and to those who need compassionate loving care.*"

In our world of healthcare, patients and family members are most often struggling with fear, pain, uncertainty, loss, sadness and even tragedy. That is why I believe that the purpose of healthcare is twofold – to meet the medical and emotional needs of the patient and the family. It is during these defining moments that caregivers provide expert medical care. It is also critical that hearts are offered through empathy and compassion in the midst of our patient's battle. Empathy allows us to connect with patients and their family members by putting ourselves in their place and opening our heart to feel what they are experiencing. Compassion is love in action. It is the choice to make a difference by sacrificing personal comfort and convenience in order to help relieve the suffering of another.

There are so many who have made the choice to serve others and to be a "*healing presence*" for patients and their families - nurses, CNAs, physicians, advanced practice providers, volunteers, ancillary staff, etc. The work is demanding, emotionally exhausting, and never ending. There is personal pain and sacrifice involved in compassionate caring and this is where heroes are found. There is nothing to compare to the splendor and worth of unselfishly serving others with compassion – this is our life's calling in healthcare. Always remember, as a caregiver, you have chosen a life of giving, a life of serving and a life of providing comfort to those in need.

Remember, creating and delivering a culture that is strategy focused includes an environment where the patients are center stage. There has been an increased interest in and focus on improving the patient experience in hospitals, health systems and clinics around the nation due in large part to the reimbursement implications resulting from the Value Based Purchasing model developed by the Centers for Medicare and Medicaid Services.

Additionally, patient loyalty and the resulting word of mouth positive advertising have a direct impact on the bottom-line. Conversely, patients who have a negative experience can broadcast, through social media platforms, to hundreds of other existing and potential patients. As pointed out earlier from The Group Practice Journal "Healthcare customers rely on personal recommendations from family and friends to judge an organization's quality of healthcare more than any other source of information."

Also consider how consumers expectations have been shaped by other businesses out-side of the healthcare industry related to cycle-time, service, experience, cost and quality. Companies that do this best earn our business and loyalty. The expectations of healthcare consumers will only continue to increase when they have to pay more for healthcare out of their own pocket. The patient experience paradigm has arrived and is here to stay and an Awakened Organization acknowledges and embraces this reality.

I have defined the patient experience as: The patients' perception of their experience driven by the behavior of the people in the organization, which influences the quality of all interactions from before the patient arrives until after the patient leaves and every touch-point in-between. I believe that compassionate people, caring for people is essential to meeting a patient's and their family's medical and emotional needs and that care practices should be organized around the needs and priorities of the patients and families – this is what an Awakened Healthcare Organization does.

A patient first orientation should remind us that a patient lying in a bed signifies an illness that needs treatment, a physiological problem that needs a solution and an emotional needs that needs kindness. The analytical nature of health care requires all of us to stay focused on the clinical and support needs necessary to effectively care for our patients. However, it is essential that we cannot ever forget that the person we are caring for is much more than a diagnosis. Each patient has stories, personal histories, disappointments and achievements.

Compassion is so important because the person in the bed is more than a patient. They are a mother, a daughter, a son, a father; they are a grandparent, a grandchild, a husband, a wife, or a close friend. It's not easy to be involved with other people's pain because it can get messy and sometimes it brings us to tears as well. You may get burned out and exhausted at times, but this is at the core of what we must do because the person in the bed is more than a patient.

As healthcare professionals, we need to continuously strive to deliver the best patient experience, which includes quality care, access, responsiveness, safety and compassion. There may never be enough time to learn about the lives and histories of each patient, but as we work every day and night, we are caring for people who have made an impact on others, who are loved by others and who have life histories beyond illness, ailments and disease.

I submit this challenge - imagine that the person in the bed is the person you love most in the world, and when you do, the person in the bed will be more than a patient to you.

While becoming an Awakened Organization is something we all wish to achieve, implementing the needed elements in the model is a demanding task particularly when battling the day-to-day urgent demands. Using the Awakened Organization Model without the knowledge and know-how can be difficult and frustrating. The intent in writing this book was to help guide you through the journey by providing a roadmap along with practical insights, guideposts and tools. Creating a truly exceptional organization is not for the faint-hearted; it requires steadfast discipline, unwavering commitment and an understanding there is no end to the work because the strategy, culture, people, and processes require daily nurturing. This book lays the foundation to support awakening your organization to the incredible opportunities that await you.

Appendix

Questions to Consider

Clear Consistent Direction	Strategy Supportive Culture	High Performing People	Continuous Process Improvement
1. Do we have a compelling organizational purpose?	1. Is your culture aligned or misaligned to supporting the strategic agenda of the organization?	1. How often do we compromise on staffing with high performing people and why?	1. How does senior leadership need to show up differently to ensure process improvement success?
2. What our promises to our patients and to each other?	2. Are the core values of the organization born from the beliefs that everyone must embody to live the purpose, deliver on the promises, and achieve the goals?	2. How do we consider the complexity of a function when appointing talent?	2. What are the processes that matter most in our organization that need to be improved?
3. What is our vision and does everyone understand it?	3. Have a handful of essential behaviors been identified for each core value?	3. Have we been deliberate in appointing A-Level talent to complex departments?	3. Who are the ultimate customers of the processes that matter most?
4. Are our vision and goals expressed from A to B by when?	4. How healthy and fit is the organization's culture within the contest of strategy execution?	4. What hiring practices do we use?	4. Who are the right people to involve in the process improvement efforts?
5. Do the goals advance us closer to achieving the vision?	5. What current signals help and hinder progress?	5. What would it be like in our organization if everyone mastered the STAR technique?	5. How do we keep the approach simple enough for people to understand and relevant enough to scale once successful?
6. Do we have the right strategies to accomplish the goals?	6. What role does mood play in the style of the organization's culture?	6. What is our Culture Quotient and what should we do to improve it?	6. What change management approach will be used to ensure key stakeholders accept and buy-in to the process change?
7. Do we have goal and strategy owners?	7. How do transformation rate limiting factors show up and how will are they mitigated?	7. How does our leadership style affect the mood of our people?	7. How does the current structure of the organization help and hinder optimum process performance?
8. Are detailed work plans developed outlining the implementation plan of the strategies?	8. Is a rigorous and disciplined approach used to navigate the culture transformation process?	8. Do we know who the Woodpeckers are and are we willing to deal with them?	
9. How can we use Line of Sights to align departments and individuals to their part to play in the strategic plan accomplishment?		9. Have we analyzed and adjusted signals to align to the culture we are trying to create?	
10. Have we articulated values that enable strategy execution?		10. How well do our training, education, and career development reinforce the core values and essential behaviors?	
11. Does everyone understand they have three primary responsibilities?		11. What recognition practices do our leaders use to express sincere appreciation to our employees?	

Appendix

The Awakened Organization Model

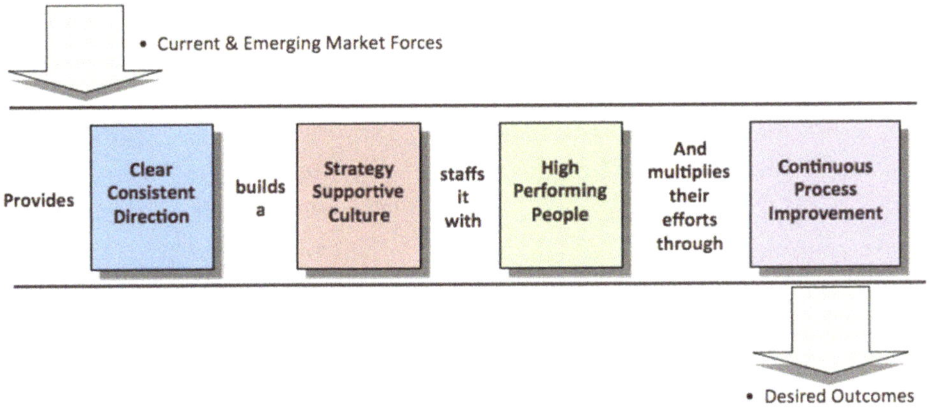

Strategic Planning System

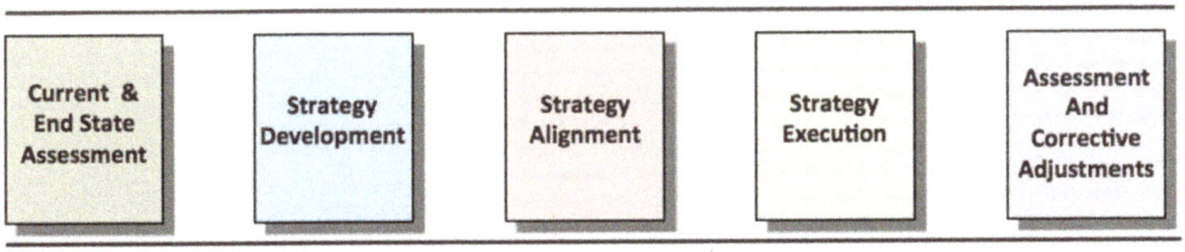

Appendix

The Difference Between Strategic and Operational Planning

Strategic Planning	Operational Planning
• Focuses on the future – and then determines what must be done in the present to achieve the future. • Top-Down: leaders spending time in the future to identify market forces and the likely impact. • Considers changes in the market environment – social, technical, economic, political, competitive.	• Begins with the present – what we do well and not well – and focuses on how we can improve. • Bottom-Up: people closest to the work know what needs to be improved and how. • Focuses on the organizations internal structure, traditions, and practices.

Strategic Plan Tree Diagram

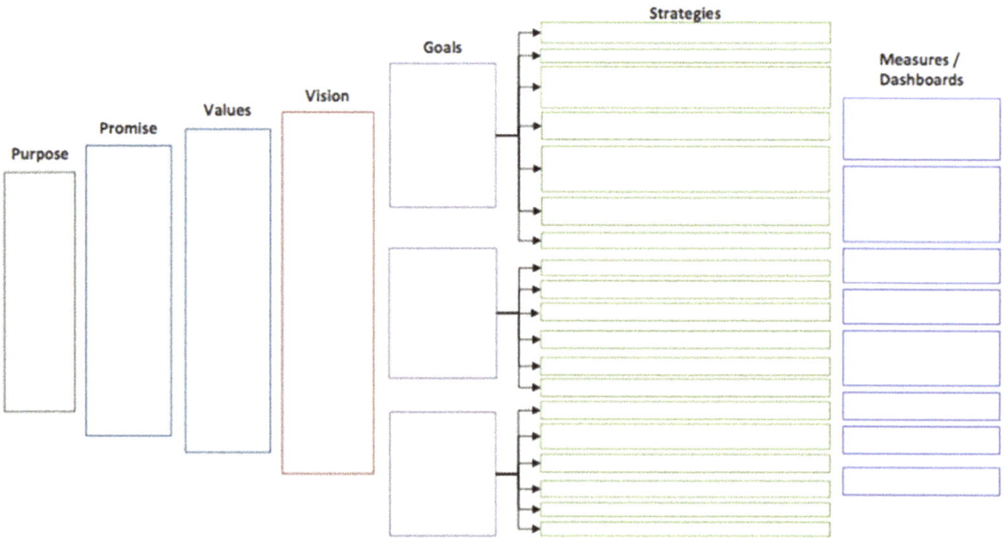

Appendix

SWOT Analysis

Area of Focus: Cardiology

Our Current State Assessment			
Our Strengths	Our Weaknesses	Our Opportunities	Our Threats

Primary Competition

Competition Current State Assessment			
Their Strengths	Their Weaknesses	Their Opportunities	Their Threats

Appendix

Strategic Plan Summary

Purpose			
Promise			
Vision			
Goal 1	Goal 2	Goal 3	Goal 4
Strategies	Strategies	Strategies	Strategies
Value 1	Value 2	Value 3	Value 4
Behaviors	Behaviors	Behaviors	Behaviors

Appendix

Strategy Action Planning Tool

Strategy:			
Tactic	Owner	Due Date	Deliverables
Key Dependencies:			

Part-to-Play

Organizational Goal	Department Contribution	My Contribution

Appendix

Part-to-Play Example

Human Resource Function

Organizational Goal	Department Contribution	My Contribution
Grow outpatient market share from 15% to 20% in 18 months.	1. Complete needs assessment to determine support needed from HR to support the growth target 2. Update HR plan to support staffing needs of growth target	a. Administer needs assessment and develop report outlining needed HR support
Move from a 3 star to a 4 star rating in HCAHPS in 18 months.	1. Provide education and training on patient experience improvement 2. Provide coaching to staff who interact with patients and family members 3. Assess and improve the culture of targeted departments	a. Design the patient experience improvement curriculum b. Administer a culture assessment and develop culture readiness report
Open the new Rehabilitation Hospital in the summer of 2019	1. Develop a workforce plan to staff the new hospital 2. Recruit, select and onboard the leadership team for the new hospital 3. Recruit, select, and onboard staff for the new hospital	a. Identify the staffing needs for the new hospital b. Source and recruit people to fill the staffing needs c. Provide candidates to hiring leader
Expand primary care services from 243 employed physicians to 363 employed physicians in 24 months	1. Develop total compensation model for new physicians 2. Develop the employment contract for new physicians 3. Onboard new physicians	a. Develop the employment contract and review and finalize with the Legal Department

Healthy and Fit Cultures

Healthy and Fit Culture	Unhealthy and Unfit Culture
• Low turnover from high performers • Higher percentage of engaged versus disengaged employees • Signals aligned to the declared values • No boundaries • Minimal politics • People focus on what matters most to the organization • High energy and contagious enthusiasm • Flow of innovation and ideas • High productivity • People are optimistic and open hearted • Solution orientation mindset	• High turnover from high performers • Higher percentage of disengaged versus engaged employees • Signals misaligned to the declared values • Many silos • High degree of politics • People focus on what matters most to them • Low energy and contagious negativity • Innovation and ideas stifled • Low productivity • Lower mood states • Problem oriented

Appendix

Patient Experience Touch-Points

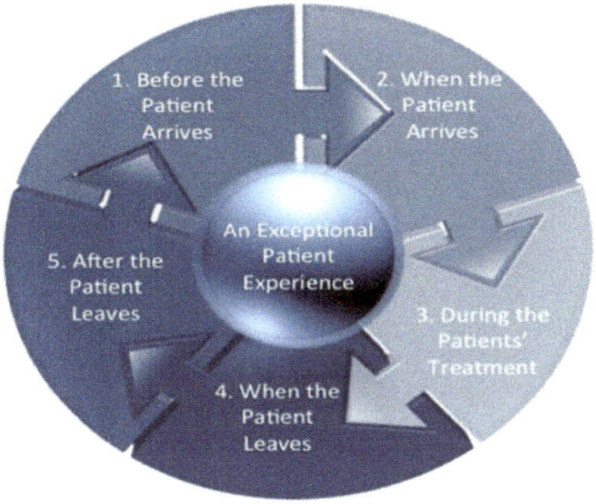

Old and New Paradigms

Old Paradigm	New Paradigm
• Leadership style direct command/control	• Leadership style of stewardship & inclusion
• Behavior will change with a tell approach	• Behavior will change when those closest to the work are part of the solution
• Initiative overload	• A model of focus and discipline
• Leadership model non inclusive of physicians	• Dyad leadership model
• The importance of IQ	• Importance of EQ
• Care team centric	• Patient centric
• Focus on volume	• Focus on value
• Focus is on fixing the patient experience	• Focus is on fixing the culture by connecting the hearts, minds and souls of care team and patient experience naturally happens
• We can rehabilitate everyone	• Not everyone is coachable

Appendix

Shifting Thinking and Behaviors

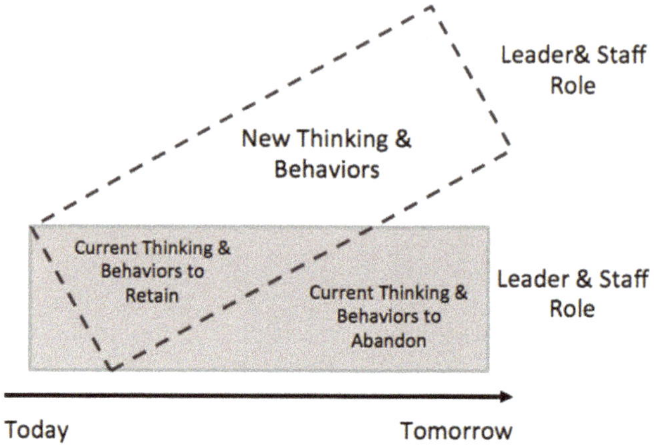

Culture Transformation Process

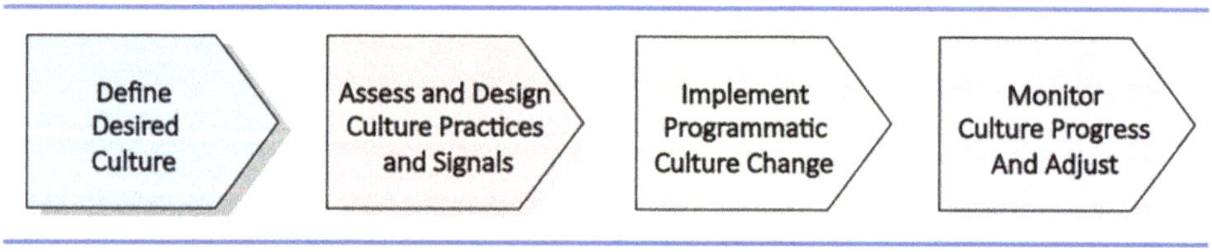

- Reflect on the purpose, promise, vision, and goals
- Define the beliefs that employees need to embody to support the purpose, promise, vision, and goals
- Develop the values based on the declared beliefs
- Identify the non negotiable behaviors for each value
- Take baseline assessment of defined desired culture

- Assess and design solutions for the following practices and signals:
  - Leadership
  - Hiring
  - System Orientation
  - Department Orientation
  - Training & Education
  - Coaching
  - Talent Management
  - Accountability
  - Performance Management
  - Recognition & Rewards
  - Communication
  - Policies
  - Mood

- Identify target areas for initial rollout
- Create Culture Transformation Steering Committee and Project Teams
- Launch project teams to implement solutions
- Meet frequently with project teams to monitor progress and make corrective adjustments
- Use change management practices to enlist and engage key stakeholders
- Hardwire the STAR technique

- Track results against desired targets
- Make visible by regularly communicating progress
- Celebrate wins with rewards and recognition for achieving targets
- Conduct frequent After Action Reviews
- Reassess culture annually

Appendix

Culture Quotient

	Culture Quotient									
	Rating Scale									
	Never	Rarely		Sometimes				Freqently		Always
Behavior Statements	1	2	3	4	5	6	7	8	9	10

Woodpeckers

Appendix

Behaviors to Start, Stop, Continue

Behaviors I need to Start	Behaviors I need to Stop	Behaviors I need to Continue

Complexity of Function

	Complexity of Function				
	Rating Scale				
	Never	Rarely	Sometimes	Freqently	Always
Behavior Statements	1	2	3	4	5
Leader has large span of control/responsible for a large number of people					
Function experiences high patient volumes					
Function responsible for contributing to the financial success of the organization					
Function is highly political					
Function is highly regulated					
Function has a matrixed organizational structure					
People in the function have to work at a fast pace					
Shelf life of key practices (technology/equipment/supplies) is short					
Evidence based medical practices change frequently					
Comlexity of patient condition is high requiring very specialized skills					

Sample Accountability Standards Form

Sample Accountability Standard Form

Employee Name:		**Evaluator Name:**	
Job Title:		**Department:**	

Patient Quality: Reduce SEPSIS Mortality Rate.	**Weight**	**Evaluation**	**Performance**
• Exceeds Standard: Below CMS National Benchmark • Meets Standard: At CMS National Benchmark • Does Not Meet Standard: Above CMS National Benchmark	25%	☐ Exceeds (1.0) ☐ Meets (.5) ☐ Does Not Meet (0)	
Patient Experience: Achieve HCAHPS top box score.	**Weight**	**Evaluation**	**Performance**
• Exceeds Standard: ≥ 85% top box score on RN communication • Meets Standard: Between 82% - 84% top box on RN communication • Does Not Meet Standard: Below 82% top box on RN communication	25%	☐ Exceeds (1.0) ☐ Meets (.5) ☐ Does Not Meet (0)	
Employee Engagement: Increase ratio of engaged to disengaged employees.	**Weight**	**Evaluation**	**Performance**
• Exceeds Standard: 40% engaged employees • Meets Standard: 35% - 39% engaged employees • Does Not Meet Standard: Below 35% engaged employees	20%	☐ Exceeds (1.0) ☐ Meets (.5) ☐ Does Not Meet (0)	
Department Finance: Achieve at or below department budget for the year.	**Weight**	**Evaluation**	**Performance**
• Exceeds Standard: 2.0% or more below budget • Meets Standard: Equal to or up to 1.99% below budget • Does Not Meet Standard: Over budget	10%	☐ Exceeds (1.0) ☐ Meets (.5) ☐ Does Not Meet (0)	
Essential Behaviors: Consistently demonstrates the essential behaviors.	**Weight**	**Evaluation**	**Performance**
• Makes eye contact, smiles, and greets the patient • Escorts patient and family members to their destination • Washes hands when entering and leaving a patient room • Makes a personal connection with the patient • Provide a gentle touch on the patient hand or shoulder	20%	☐ Exceeds (1.0) ☐ Meets (.5) ☐ Does Not Meet (0)	

Appendix

Sample Interview Guide

Interview Guide

Candidate Name	Interview Date:
Job Applied: Chief Medical Officer	Interviewer Name:

Interview Questions	Rating Scale 1 Does not meet expectations	 2 Meets expectations	 3 Exceeds expectations
1. Please tell me what has happened during the day at work when you go home feeling really good and feeling really bad. Notes:	☐	☐	☐
2. Please tell me how you have engaged and aligned physicians to something strategically or operationally important. Notes:	☐	☐	☐
3. Please tell me about dyad or triad relationships you have built. Notes:	☐	☐	☐
4. Please tell about what you believe about organizational culture? Notes:	☐	☐	☐
5. Please tell me what role you have played in fostering a patient centric culture. Notes:	☐	☐	☐
6. Please tell what you believe are the most important factors that drive a patient's experience from their perspective. Notes:	☐	☐	☐
7. Please tell me about what you believe about employee engagement. Notes:	☐	☐	☐
8. Please tell me how you have improved employee engagement. Notes:	☐	☐	☐
9. What was your last boss's name? Tell me about NAME. When I talk with NAME, what will he/she tell me your strengths and limitations? Notes:	☐	☐	☐
10. Please tell me what you are deeply passionate about at work. Notes:	☐	☐	☐
11. Please tell me about the most difficult change you had to lead. What made it difficult and what was the outcome? Notes:	☐	☐	☐
Overall Assessment *(Complete sections below at conclusion of interview)*			
Leadership Competence/Presence	☐	☐	☐
Compassionate Attitude	☐	☐	☐
Culture Aptitude	☐	☐	☐
Overall Assessment	☐	☐	☐

Recommended Decision: ☐ Hire ☐ Don't Hire

Appendix

Sample Whiteboard

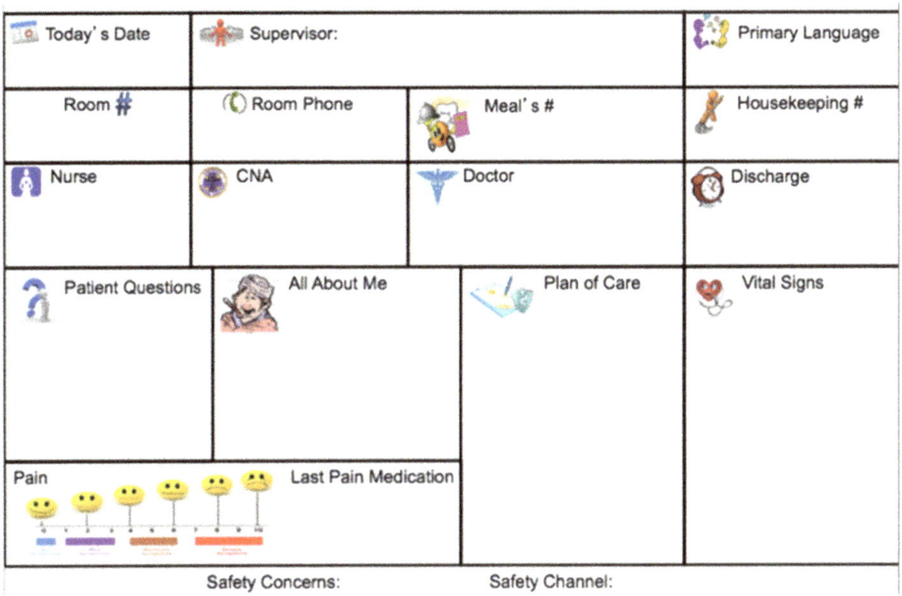

5P Worksheet

The change to be managed:	Insert here

5 Ps	What Will I Communication for This Change
1. Purpose • The reason for the change. Why does this need to happen? • What is the problem? What is the evidence to support the problem? • What would occur if no one acts to solve it?	
2. Picture • The vivid description of the desired state • What will the outcome look like? • How will it feel to be a participant in the outcome? • What is the What's In It For Me (WIIFM) for staff?	
3. Plan • What is the plan to get from here to there? • What is the timeline? What are the goals? • What are the key steps?	
4. Part to Play • My role – my responsibilities • How do I fit into this scheme? • What is my role? • How will my job change?	
5. Prize/Penalty • Describe the consequences • What is the upside of the change? • What is the downside of the change?	

Bibliography

[1] Codler, Estelle, and David d. Codier. Could Emotional Intelligence Make Patients Safer, American Journal of Nursing, July 2017.

[2] The Healing Power of Kindness, Dignity Health and Stanford University's Center for Compassion and Altruism Research and Education.

[3] Collins, James C. Good to Great: Why Some Companies Make the Leap...and Others Don't, William Collins, 2001.

[4] HealthCast 2020: Creating a Sustain- able Future. PricewaterhouseCoopers. 2006. Available at: www.pwc.com/us/ eng/about/ind/healthcare/hc2020. html.

[5] ***"The Sad End Of Blockbuster Video: The Onetime $5 Billion Company Is Being Liquidated As Competition From Online Giants Netflix And Hulu Prove All Too Much For The Iconic Brand"****. International Business Times. 5 December 2013.*

[6] ***"Blockbuster LLC Chapter 11 Petition"*** *(PDF). PacerMonitor. PacerMonitor. Retrieved 9 May 2016.*

[7] ***"DISH Network Completes Acquisition of Blockbuster Assets"****. DishNetwork.MediaRoom.com. April 26, 2011. Retrieved June 16, 2011.*

[8] Miles, Robert H. Corporate Transformation Resources, LLC

[9] Kaplan, Robert S., and David P. Norton. The Strategy-Focused Organization: How Balanced Scorecard Companies Thrive in the New Business Environment. Harvard Business Press, 2000.

[10] Kryscynski, David What is Strategy,
https://www.youtube.com/watch?v=TD7WSLeQtVw
Brigham Young University Marriott School of Management and the Center for Teaching & Learning, 2012.

[11] Drain, M., & Kaldenberg, D.O., "Building patient loyalty and trust: The role of patient satisfaction." Group Practice Journal. 1999.

[12] Collins, James C., and Jerry I. Porras. Built to Last: Successful Habits of Visionary Companies, HarperBusiness, 1994.

[13] McChesney, Chris, Sean Covey, and Jim Huling. The 4 Disciplines of Execution: Achieving Your Wildly Important Goals, Simon and Schuster, 2012.

[14] How to Build a High Performing Organization, American Management Association, 2007.

[15] Diering, Scott, L. M.D., "Love Your Patients." Blue Dolphin Publishing. 2004.

[16] Miles, Robert H. Accelerating Corporate Transformation (Don't Lose Your Nerve). Harvard Business Review, 2009.

[17] Nerburn, Kent "The Cab Ride I'll Never Forget." From Make Me an Instrument of Your Peace: Living in the Spirit of the Prayer of St. Francis. Published by HarperOne. 2013.

[18] Collins, James C. Good to Great: Why Some Companies Make the Leap...and Others Don't, William Collins, 2001.

[19] Kruse, Kevin, "The ROI of Employee Engagement in Hospitals." Forbes. 2015.

[20] "State of the Global Workplace Report." Gallup Organization. 2013.

[21] Barker, Joel Leadershift: 5 Lessons for Leaders in the 21st Century, Star Thrower Distribution, 1999.

[22] Barker, Joel Leadershift: 5 Lessons for Leaders in the 21st Century, Star Thrower Distribution, 1999.

[23] *Brown, Barrett C., "The Future of Leadership for Conscious Capitalism." MetaIntegral Associates. 2013.*

[24] *Gostick, Adrian and Chester Elton. The Carrot Principle, Free Press, 2007.*

[25] *Rath, Tom, and Donald O. Clifton, "How Full is Your Bucket." The Gallup Organization. 2004.*

[26] *Sisney, Lex. The 5 Classic Mistakes in Organizational Structure: Or, How to Design Your Organization the Right Way, Web Post, 2012.*

[27] *Fox, Paula J., "Heart of a Caregiver: Touching Lives with Compassion and Care." Simple Truths L.L.C. 2011.*

About the Author

Brad Pollins, MS, SPHR

Brad is a passionate change leader who is committed to transforming healthcare organizations into becoming patient-centric, change adaptive, and world-class care providers.

He has 35 years of professional experience and has expertise in organizational effectiveness, strategic planning, change management, culture transformation, patient experience improvement, employee engagement, and leadership talent development. Brad has worked in a variety of industries including consulting, manufacturing, consumer products, utilities, insurance, telecommunications, and food service. He has been a key member of corporate leadership teams providing strategic and operational insights.

During the past 24 years, Brad has worked in healthcare where he led programs to transform the culture to achieve better strategic and operational outcomes.

He developed and led the organizational development function for a large, multifaceted and highly integrated healthcare system. He has received a number of recognitions including the President's Circle Award for Employee Engagement and he helped lead people practices that resulted in achieving Employer of Choice and Premier Healthcare Employer Awards.

He has also been sought-after facilitator of strategic planning, patient experience improvement, organizational development and performance improvement efforts.

Brad has a Master's degree in Industrial and Organizational Psychology from the University of Central Florida, a Bachelor's of Arts Degree in Psychology from the Florida State University, and has completed the Florida Sterling Council and Malcolm Baldrige examiner training.

He is natural leader who triggers the best instincts in others and deeply believes that the physics of performance lies within the people.

Brad is married with four children and lives in Estero, Florida, U.S.A.